THE STORY OF A CIVIL CASE:
DOMINGUEZ V. SCOTT'S FOOD STORES, INC.

THIRD EDITION

BY
DAVID CRUMP

NEWELL H. BLAKELY PROFESSOR OF LAW,
UNIVERSITY OF HOUSTON LAW CENTER

AND
JEFFREY B. BERMAN

ASSOCIATE DEAN
AND
PROFESSOR OF LAW,
UNIVERSITY OF MISSOURI AT KANSAS CITY

THE JOHN MARSHALL PUBLISHING COMPANY
C/O DAVID CRUMP
UNIVERSITY OF HOUSTON LAW CENTER
100 LAW CENTER
HOUSTON, TEXAS 77204-6060
(713) 743-2069

ISBN 0-916081-03-6

Printed in the United States of America.

Second printing, 1984. The second printing is identical to the first with correction of typographical and layout errors.

Second edition, 1985.

Third edition, 2001.

TABLE OF CONTENTS

CHAPTER ONE:
WHAT THIS BOOK IS ABOUT

A. THE CASE: DOMINGUEZ V. SCOTT'S FOOD STORES, INC.   1
B. WHERE THE CASE CAME FROM   1
C. WHY THIS BOOK WILL BE USEFUL TO YOU   2

CHAPTER TWO:
DOCUMENTS GENERATED BEFORE SUIT

A. THE CLAIMS ADJUSTER'S FILE   3
    Cover Letter   3
    Witness Report   4
    Claimant's Statement   4
    Diagram of Scene   5
    Adjuster's Evaluation   5
    Final Letter   6
B. NOTES AND QUESTIONS ON THE CLAIMS ADJUSTER'S FILE   6
C. THE PLAINTIFF'S ATTORNEY'S INITIAL FILE   7
    Plaintiff's Attorney's Notes of First Interview   7
    Employment Agreement Used by Plaintiff's Attorney   8
    Medical Authorization   9
    Demand Letter   9
    Note on Obtaining of Medical Narrative Summary   10
    Narrative Summary From Plaintiff's Physician   11
D. NOTES AND QUESTIONS ON PLAINTIFF'S ATTORNEY'S INITIAL FILE   13

CHAPTER THREE:
PLEADINGS, DISCOVERY, AND INITIAL PRETRIAL PROCEEDINGS

A. SUMMONS, COMPLAINT, AND SERVICE   15
    Summons   15
    Complaint   16
    Note on Service and Return   18
B. DEFENDANT'S ATTACK ON THE COMPLAINT   19
    Defendant's Rule 12 Motion   19
C. NOTES AND QUESTIONS ON INITIAL PLEADINGS AND ORDER   20
D. EARLY CONFERENCE AND SETTLEMENT EFFORTS   21
    Initial Pretrial Conference   21
    Order Resulting From Pretrial Conference   23
E. DISCOVERY   24
    Plaintiff's Request For Admissions and Defendant's Answers   24
    Note on Agreement For Deposition Schedule   25
    Deposition of Plaintiff   25

F. NOTES AND QUESTIONS ON DISCOVERY   31

G. FINAL PLEADINGS: AMENDED COMPLAINT AND ANSWER   33

    Amended Complaint   33

    Answer on the Merits   34

H. NOTES ON FINAL PLEADINGS   36

ADDENDUM TO CHAPTER THREE   36

I. MOTION FOR SUMMARY JUDGMENT   36

    Defendant's Motion For Summary Judgment   37

    Defendant's Brief in Support of Motion For Summary Judgment   37

    Plaintiff's Brief in Opposition to Summary Judgment   39

    Note on Court's Order Denying Summary Judgment   40

J. NOTES AND QUESTIONS ON MOTION FOR SUMMARY JUDGMENT   40

CHAPTER FOUR:
LATER PRETRIAL PROCEEDINGS

A. JOINT PRETRIAL ORDER PROPOSAL   41

    The Draft Pretrial Order   41

B. THE PROCESS OF SCHEDULING THE CASE FOR TRIAL   44

    Note on Setting the Case For Trial   44

    First Trial Setting Request Form   44

    Note on Multiple Resetting of Case For Trial   45

C. PROCEEDINGS ON THE EVE OF TRIAL   47

    Motion in Limine   47

    Proposed Order on Motion in Limine   48

    Subpoena to Medical Records Custodian   49

    Note on Pretrial Conference References to the Federal Rules of Evidence   50

    Excerpt From Transcript of Final Pretrial Hearing   50

CHAPTER FIVE:
THE TRIAL

A. JURY SELECTION   52

    Juror Information Forms of the Panel   52

    Plaintiff's Voir Dire Examination of Prospective Jurors (Excerpt From Transcript)   56

    Defendant's Voir Dire Examination of the Jury (Excerpt From Transcript)   62

    Plaintiff's Jury List and Challenges   63

    Defendant's Jury List and Challenges   63

    Clerk's Final Jury List   63

B. NOTES AND QUESTIONS REGARDING JURY SELECTION   63

C. THE TRIAL: PLAINTIFF'S EVIDENCE   64

    Transcript of the Proceedings   64

D. DEFENDANT'S MOTION FOR JUDGMENT AS MATTER OF LAW   86

Transcript of the Proceedings 86
E. NOTES AND QUESTIONS ON THE TRIAL 87
F. THE TRIAL: DEFENDANT'S EVIDENCE 88
   Transcript of the Proceedings 88
G. RENEWAL OF THE MOTION FOR JUDGMENT AS A MATTER OF LAW 91
   Note 91
H. JURY ARGUMENT 92
   Excerpts From Plaintiff's Opening Argument (From Transcript) ... 92
   Excerpts From Defendant's Jury Argument (From Transcript) 95
   Excerpts From Plaintiff's Closing Argument (From Transcript) 98
I. CHARGE AND VERDICT 99
   Note on Preparation of the Charge 99
J. OBJECTIONS TO THE CHARGE 101
   Transcript of the Proceedings 102
K. NOTES AND QUESTIONS ON COURT'S CHARGE, OBJECTIONS, AND JURY ARGUMENT 102

CHAPTER SIX:
THE POST-TRIAL STAGE AND THE APPEAL

A. JUDGMENT AND POST-TRIAL MOTIONS 104
   Note on Receipt of Verdict, Motion for Judgment, and Entry of Judgment ... 104
   Motion for Judgment as a Matter of Law 105
   Motion for New Trial 106
B. THE TAKING OF THE APPEAL 107
   Robert Livingston's Memorandum to the File Concerning Time Schedule on Appeal ... 107
   Modification of Plaintiff's Fee Contract 108
   Requests for Preparation of Record 108
   Order Overruling Post-Trial Motions 110
   Notice of Appeal 110
   Cost Bond 111
   Excerpts From Appellant's Brief 111
   Note on Plaintiff's Brief 115
C. NOTES AND QUESTIONS REGARDING POST-TRIAL MOTIONS AND APPEAL ... 115
D. THE APPELLATE COURT'S DECISION 116
   Appellate Opinion 116
   Note on Petition for Rehearing and on Mandate 118
E. THE SUPREME COURT 118
   Note on Petition for Certiorari 118
F. SATISFACTION OF THE JUDGMENT 119
   Rough Estimate of Price Paid by Defendant for Entire Litigation ... 119
   Note on Release of Judgment 119
   Closing Statement Between Plaintiff & Her Attorney 120
G. NOTES AND QUESTIONS ON THE EXPENSE OF LITIGATION ... 120

APPENDIX:
THE REAL LAWYERS IN DOMINGUEZ V. SCOTT'S FOOD STORES

THE DEFENSE LAWYER   123

THE PLAINTIFF'S LAWYER   126

THE JUDGE   128

CHAPTER ONE:

WHAT THIS BOOK IS ABOUT

A. THE CASE: DOMINGUEZ V. SCOTT'S FOOD STORES, INC.

On May 7, 1996, Ms. Miranda Dominguez went to Scott's Food Store No. 14 on Quitman Street in the City of London, State of West York, to do some shopping. Her husband, who had just returned from work, drove her to the store in their car but did not go into the store with his wife. After entering the store, Ms. Dominguez went to the area where shopping carts were kept, nested one inside the other. She pulled the first cart in one of the rows; the result was that several carts came out together. Ms. Dominguez lost her balance and fell, placing her right hand behind her as she did so.

The fall caused her a compound fracture of the arm above the wrist. Her medical and hospital bills ultimately totalled $ 1172.55. The doctor treating her estimated that she had a permanent partial disability of 10 to 15 per cent in the wrist.

This book tells the story of the suit that was precipitated by that incident.

B. WHERE THE CASE CAME FROM

The book is based on the actual lititgation in J. Weingarten, Inc. v. Obiedio, 515 S.W.2d 308 (Tex. Civ. App.—Houston [1st Dist.] 1974, writ ref'd n.r.e.). The litigation has been transformed into a diversity suit taking place in the mythical United States District Court for the Middle District of West York. These changes have required redrafting of the formal parts of certain documents, such as the summons and complaint. However, the "business" parts of these documents remain close to the original.

Certain procedures remain undocumented in every lawsuit. Settlement negotiations, the claims adjuster's file, and similar matters are generally unavailable. The voir dire examination of prospective jurors and the argument were never transcribed here because they presented no appellate issues. In each instance, the procedure in question was reconstructed, with interviews of the attorneys furnishing a guide wherever possible.

The evidence is taken directly from the trial transcript, and the result is the same as that returned by the real jury. Thus, even though parts of what you are about to read are reconstructed or simulated, we believe they faithfully reproduce the nature of the proceedings.

C. WHY THIS BOOK WILL BE USEFUL TO YOU

This is a very ordinary case. It is not a landmark. It makes no new points of law, and it is unlikely to grace the pages of a law school book (except, of course, this one). But that is exactly why it is likely to be useful to you. It will show you prototypical procedure in a prototypical case, from beginning to end, with every important document laid out before you.

The cases in your casebooks are not typical. In general, each one turns upon a single issue or set of issues that is complex and unusual; that is why it has been chosen for a casebook. Those cases are, for the most part, cases that "make" the law. They make you look at each legal principle through a microscope. But microscopes can be confining, and it is hoped that this little book will help you place that view in context.

Furthermore, it would be a mistake to underestimate this humble case. It provides material for endless debate about the strategy of jury selection, about the controversies of pleading, and about methods of deposition questioning. And when the strategy debate on such matters ends, this case provides the basis for deeper, more philosophical discussions. For example, should attorneys conduct voir dire examination, or should the judge? (Do the attorneys do a better job of detecting prejudice, or does attorney voir dire just mean that the trial starts with a showboating personality contest that demeans the process for discovering truth?) How should an attorney approach a witness who is attempting to tell the truth, but is confused? What part should the pleadings really play in the trial? (Should there be more stringent requirements of specificity? Or should details be obtained through discovery?) Finally, what about the enormous cost of litigation in such suits as this, exceeding the amount in controversy? Should our system devise means for dispute resolution that are cheaper—both for the parties, and for society? A study of this case provides fresh insight into such issues.

D. THE THIRD EDITION

The third edition of this book has been updated to reflect changes in rules, especially those governing pleadings and sanctions. Cost data are converted to estimates for the year 2000 (although the jury's damage finding remains unaltered). Details conform more closely to contemporary events and practice, and the date of the accident is transformed from 1969 to 1996, with other dates advanced by the same period. Still, this edition remains closely similar to the first and second, and it faithfully represents the case upon which it is based.

CHAPTER TWO:

DOCUMENTS GENERATED BEFORE SUIT

A. THE CLAIMS ADJUSTER'S FILE

COVER LETTER

XYZ CLAIM COMPANY
ADJUSTERS
300 10TH STREET
LONDON, WEST YORK 77002

Mr. Tom Ball   May 27, 1996
Scott's Food Stores
505 Robbins Place
London, West York   Re: Ms. Miranda Dominguez
                                Our Claim no. 69-4316

Dear Mr. Ball:

    As per your request of May 10, 1996, we have investigated
the above captioned claim. We have further notified the doctor
that initial bills should be referred for payment to us. We
attach a scene diagram and statements of claimant and others
who were present. The only others present known to us were the
store manager and assistant manager. Please advise as to
settlement authority.

                            Very truly yours,
                            XYZ CLAIM COMPANY

                            Karl W. Stonebreaker
                            Karl W. Stonebreaker

WITNESS REPORT

Name **ERATH PITTSTON** Position **ASST. MGR.**

Reason for Presence **ON DUTY AT THE TIME**

State What You Saw **WAS IN BACK OF STORE, SAW COMMOTION, CAME FRONT, SAW LADY WITH BROKEN WRIST**

State What Other Persons Told You Happened **LADY, MS. DOMINGUEZ, STATED PULLED CART, LOST BALANCE, + FELL**

Other Known Witnesses **SEVERAL PEOPLE BUT NO NAMES**

Describe Injury **BROKEN WRIST**

State What, if Any, Treatment for First Aid Used **TAKEN TO HOSPITAL BY HUSBAND**

Remarks _____

Signature *Erath A Pittston*

CLAIMANT'S STATEMENT

Name **MIRANDA DOMINGUEZ** Address **2944 DUNHAM**

Husband or Wife Name **EDWARD** Telephone **666-1011**

Occupation **HOUSEWIFE** Age **58**

Place of Birth **MEXICO** Next of Kin **EDWARD (HUSB).**

Purpose for Visiting Store **BUY A FEW THINGS**

Date of Injury, if Any **5/7/96** Store Location **QUITMAN**

Claimant's Statement of How Injury Occurred **I PULLED ON A BASKET BUT IT WAS STUCK AND ALL BASKETS CAME OUT, KNOCKED ME DOWN**

Treatment/First Aid **HUSBAND TOOK TO HOSPITAL**

Hospital **MEMORIAL** Doctor **ELLMAN, RALPH M.D.**

Describe Injury Fully **BROKEN WRIST OR ARM WITH BONE STICKING OUT**

Who Else Saw Accident? **NAMES UNKNOWN**

Social Security Number **606-42-1017** Driver's Lic. **2221467**

State What, in Your Opinion, Caused Accident **BASKET WAS STUCK TO ALL THE OTHER BASKETS**

Have You Ever Had an Injury to This Area of Body Before? **NO**

Have You Ever Been a Party to a Lawsuit or Made a Claim? **YES**

Explain **HURT LEG IN FALL IN ANOTHER SCOTT'S FOOD STORE + SETTLED WITHOUT SUIT**

Signature *Miranda Dominguez*

Person Taking Statement **KWS**

Date **6/20/96**

4

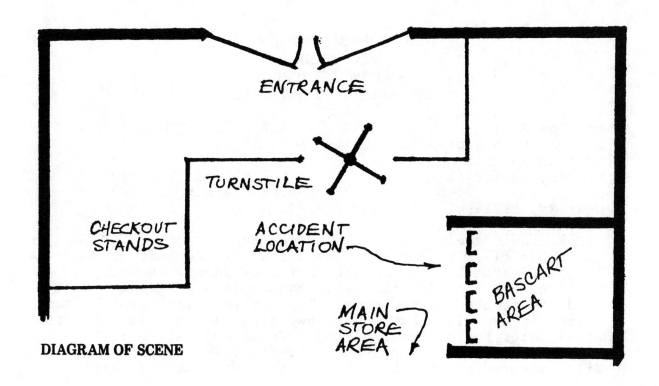

DIAGRAM OF SCENE

Entrance

Turnstile

Checkout Stands

Accident Location

Main Store Area

Bascart Area

ADJUSTER'S EVALUATION

Claimant   MIRANDA DOMINGUEZ   Claim No. 69-4316

Date/Accident   5/7/96   Store Location   QUITMAN

Medical   DR. R. ELLMAN, AUTHORIZATION REC'D. $1172.00

Claim Probable (✓)Yes __ No __ Indeterminate

Liability Probable __ Yes __ No __ (Indeterminate ✓)

Reserve Requested   OUT-OF-POCKET MEDICAL

Remarks   THIS LADY ALREADY MADE A CLAIM ONCE BEFORE FOR A SLIP-FALL IN A SCOTT'S STORE + RECEIVED A SETTLEMENT

By   KWS

5

FINAL LETTER

XYZ CLAIM COMPANY
ADJUSTERS
300 10TH STREET
LONDON, WEST YORK 77002

Mr. Tom Ball   4 February 1998
Scott's Food Stores
505 Robbins Place
London, West York   Re: Ms. Miranda Dominguez
                                          Our Claim No. 69-4316

Dear Mr. Ball:

      We have received a final medical report from Dr. Ellman in
the above claim situation. The doctor states that claimant has
10-15% disability as a result of the accident. Summary
would be a Colles fracture with causalgia and carpal tunnel
syndrome of the median nerve. The claimant was hospitalized
initially overnight but due to swelling had to return to hospital later for a longer period. Total medical is $1172.55.
      Claimant is now represented by attorney Stephen T. Elder.
Will attempt settlement with him pursuant to authorization.

                                    Very truly yours,
                                    XYZ CLAIM COMPANY

                                    Karl W. Stonebreaker
                                    Karl W. Stonebreaker

B. NOTES AND QUESTIONS ON THE CLAIMS ADJUSTER'S FILE

1. THE CLAIMS ADJUSTER'S ROLE. It is not unusual for a claims adjusting service employed by the insurer or defendant to investigate a potential dispute and (if appropriate, with the consent of the potential defendant) attempt settlement. Some entities with many claims employ full-time investigators or adjusters. The adjuster may attempt disposition of the claim with the claimant directly if no attorney represents the claimant, or may attempt settlement with an attorney.

You have probably noticed that the adjuster has gone about his work, here, differently than an attorney would. What would an attorney have done differently and perhaps better? Has the adjuster shown good performance? (Hint: What is the adjuster trying to do? And at what cost? Does the adjuster know enough to make a settlement recommendation?)

2. IS THE CLAIM FILE CONFIDENTIAL? Federal Rule 26(b)(3) provides limited protection for "trial preparation" materials. Items "prepared in anticipation of litigation or for trial by or for another party or by or for that other party's representative" are discoverable by an opponent only upon a showing of "substantial need" and "undue hardship." The Rule codifies what is known as the "work product" principle.

Can the claim file be kept confidential under this provision? If it were subject to disclosure, what would be the effect upon the decision to prepare such materials—and upon settlement?

3. SETTLEMENT. Is this a case that "ought" to be settled? For what amount, and why? In reality, defendant acted through the claims adjuster to offer the plaintiff the amount of out-of-pocket medical expenses (i.e., $ 1172.55), which plaintiff refused and her attorney later also refused on her behalf. Was this a sensible offer?

C. THE PLAINTIFF'S ATTORNEY'S INITIAL FILE

PLAINTIFF'S ATTORNEY'S NOTES OF FIRST INTERVIEW

	1234 Dunham St.
π	Ms. Miranda Dominguez 691-1041
NOK	(daughter) Thelma Rodriguez
D/A	May of '96 1820 Cody 667-1356
P/A	Scotts Food Store on Quitman
E/R	Never worked outside the Home
Facts:	slipped + fell on floor by place where baskets are
Med:	Broke her wrist
	Dr. Ralph Ellman, Bill is about
	227-2023 $1000
	1305 Spellman Professional Bldg.
	π has been contacted by a Mr. James Bryan. Said he was referring the matter to Mr. Tomball Super.

7

EMPLOYMENT AGREEMENT USED BY PLAINTIFF'S ATTORNEY

THE STATE OF WEST YORK)
)   KNOW ALL MEN BY THESE PRESENTS:

COUNTY OF MANERO)

      THAT I, _Mrs. Miranda Dominguez,_
have employed STEPHEN T. ELDER as my attorney to represent me to
prosecute through settlement or judgment certain claims I have and
hold against _____

_____
and/or any and all other persons, firms and corporations for damages
for or arising out of personal injuries to _____

_____
as well as damages to property caused by or growing out of a certain
accident which occurred on or about the _7th_ day of _May,_ ,
19_96_, _____

_____
I hereby fully authorize and empower my said attorney at law and
also in my name, place and stead to bring suits on said claims or
any of them, if necessary, and to prosecute the same to final judgment and to compromise and settle said claims or any of them with or
without suit in any way or manner that he may deem best or advisable,
giving and granting also unto my said attorney full power to substi-
tute one or more attorneys at law in his place and stead as my
attorney in or concerning the premises or any part thereof or in
the performance of any or all of the professional services hereunder
whether in the preparation of my claim or suit and whether in the
trial or appellate court, such other attorneys or attorney to be
paid by my above named attorney with no additional expense to me
by way of attorneys' fees other than hereinafter set out.

      In consideration of the services to be rendered for me by my
said attorney hereunder, I hereby sell, transfer, assign and convey
to my above named attorney or attorneys an undivided interest of
ONE THIRD (1/3) interest in and to said claims and amounts received
in settlement in the event same is or are settled without suit, and
FORTY (40%) per cent of same and of any judgments obtained or
amount received, on or for such claims or suits, if same is or are
collected by suit or by settlement after suit is filed.

      No compromise of my said claims may be made by said attorney
without my consent.

      WITNESS my hand this the _25th_ day of _January,_
_____, 19_98_.

                                       Mrs. Miranda Dominguez

MEDICAL AUTHORIZATION

TO: _____

hereby authorize and request that you allow my attorneys, _____, free access to any and all hospital and/or medical records or reports in your possession or custody and, upon request of _____, to furnish to them, at my expense, a full and complete report concerning your medical examination and treatment of _____ _____.

Mrs. Miranda Dominguez

Address: _____

DEMAND LETTER

STEPHEN T. ELDER
SUITE 412
FIRST SAVINGS BUILDING
LONDON, WEST YORK 77002

Mr. Tomball   January 27, 1998
Scott's Food Stores, Inc.
600 Lockwood
London, West York   Re: Miranda Dominguez v. Scott's
                                 Food Store, Inc.; D/A:
Dear Mr. Tomball: May, 1996

I have been retained by Mrs. Miranda Dominguez to represent her in a cause of action arising from her slipping and falling at your No. 14 Store at 1100 Quitman during May of 1996. My investigation indicates that her accident and injuries were caused by the negligence of your organization.

Should you or your liability insurance carrier desire to discuss an amicable settlement of this matter, please contact me within ten days; otherwise I shall file suit against you without further notice.

Very truly yours,

Stephen T. Elder
Stephen T. Elder

NOTE ON OBTAINING OF
MEDICAL NARRATIVE SUMMARY

On the same day he wrote the demand letter, Plaintiff's attorney wrote her physician. His letter included the following:

"I am enclosing a medical report authorization signed by Mrs. Dominguez and request that you furnish me with a narrative report concerning your diagnosis, treatment and prognosis for her injuries. I shall pay you for such report on receipt of your bill and assure the payment of any balance remaining on your fee for services rendered to Mrs. Dominguez out of any recovery she may realize.

"I wish to thank you in advance for your cooperation in this matter."

The physician responded with a letter confirming that he had indeed treated Mrs. Dominguez, but he refused to send a narrative summary. He said:

"Please be advised that reports have been rendered with copies to Scott's Food Stores, Inc., attention Mr. Tom Ball.

"Since reports have already been submitted, as above, I am referring your request directly to Scott's Food Stores for response."

Plaintiff's attorney found himself in an unenviable position. His client's physician had been reporting to the opposing party, apparently because that party had paid the doctor's intial bill. The attorney could, of course, take the doctor's deposition. But ordinarily, that would need to await the filing of suit, and it would almost certainly be a very unwise strategy since recovery would be more difficult with a hostile physician's testimony in the record.

Instead, therefore, Plaintiff's attorney simply proceeded to file his lawsuit (see the next chapter) and did nothing with respect to the physician for the time being. About five months later, having learned that the physician had sent follow-up bills to Mrs. Dominguez, Plaintiff's attorney sent Dr. Ellman the following letter:

"Mrs. Dominguez recently informed me that your office has been contacting her regularly regarding her charges. In your letter to me of February 1,1998, you declined sending me a medical report. I gathered that Scott's Foods was assuming responsibility for your bill.

"If the representatives from Scott's Food Store have changed their minds, your bill will be satisfied from the proceeds of this lawsuit."

Plaintiff's attorney's patience was rewarded. Four days after sending Dr. Ellman the letter offering to assist with his bill, plaintiff's attorney received the following detailed narrative summary.

NARRATIVE SUMMARY FROM PLAINTIFF'S PHYSICIAN

Stephen T. Elder   13 July 1998
Attorney at Law
Houston First Savings Building
London, West York

Dear Attorney Elder:

     Reference to your recent letter of July 9, 1998, regarding Mrs. Miranda
Dominguez. I greatly appreciate your very nice letter, and have reviewed the
case at this time. Review indicates that Scott's authorized and assumed
responsibility for the initial examination and report only, and declined any
further treatment thereafter. They paid the bill for the initial examination and
report, but have failed to make any payment of the subsequent charges necessary
in this case, on the basis that it was a personal injury situation, and not a
compensation type of claim. Since my responsibilities as the doctor in a
personal injury case of this type are directly to the patient, it is clearly my
medical obligation to submit the medical facts of the case to you at this time,
as per her written authorization.
     Mrs. Miranda Dominguez, a 58 year old woman, was first seen by myself on May
7, 1996, with the history that she was injured about 6:00 P.M. on the evening of
May 7, 1996, at Scott's store No. 14, when she was trying to disengage some
shopping carts, which had somehow become stuck, which jerked apart suddenly,
causing her to fall, landing heavily on her outstretched right hand and wrist,
sustaining a severe comminuted Colles' fracture of the right forearm and wrist.
I saw her at the Emergency Room at Memorial Hospital about 6:35 P.M. Examination
revealed a typical Colles' fracture deformity of the right forearm and wrist,
confirmed by x-rays, with comminution, displacement, and impaction. At that time
I performed closed anesthetic reduction of the fracture, reducing same and
immobilizing it in volar and dorsal plaster splints, admitting the patient to the
hospital overnight for observation of circulation and swelling. She was
dismissed home on May 8, 1996, doing quite well, with instructions for elevation
and control of swelling, post-fracture, as well as finger exercises and
activities. She was rechecked subsequently on May 14, 1996, at my office, with
x-rays showing maintenance of the reduction status of the fracture. At this time
the plaster splints were trimmed, and the cast completed, leaving the fingers
and thumb out for motion. Our next recheck was on May 28, 1996, with x-rays
through the cast showing the fracture to be well maintained, and showing evidence
of healing reaction progressing well. She was re-instructed in the necessity of
finger exercises at this time.
     By June 11, 1996, four weeks post-injury, she had evidence of rather marked
swelling present of the thumb and all four fingers. It was felt that this
represented both inadequate exercising by the patient and also the possibility of
a reflex causalgic syndrome, secondary to the fracture. The cast was removed
completely at this time, x-rays made which showed the reduction state to be
anatomical and excellent, and healing status to be well advanced. She was
started on hot water soaks and exercises of the hand and wrist at this time,
further instructed in elevation of the hand and wrist, as well as finger
exercising to reduce the swelling. By June 16, 1996, recheck revealed the
swelling to be still present, although subsiding, it was quite evident that this
patient had a definite complication present which occurs in an occasional
comminuted Colles' fracture of this type of severity, namely, reflex causalgic
type of condition. Because of the marked swelling existing together with the
impairment of circulation and tendency to freezing of the finger joints, she was

11

re-admitted to Memorial Hospital on June 17, 1996, and placed in marked elevation of the right hand together with appropriate exercises and other medications. With this, she showed definite improvement and the swelling subsided. Because the reflex causalgic complication was rather severe in this patient she was seen at my request by Dr. Robert A. Byrd, in consultation, Anesthesiologist, and he performed several cervical sympathetic ganglion blocks to overcome the reflex causalgia, with a good response noted to each of the blocks. She was sufficiently improved to permit dismissal home on June 23, 1996.

She was subsequently seen and followed in my office on July 16, 1996, August 6th, September 3, October 15, December 10, 1996, with progressive improvement in her condition on a slow but very definite improving basis. Because of some persistence of the reflex causalgia and tendency to develop a shoulder-band syndrome, the right shoulder was injected on September 3, 1996, with Xylocaine and Hydrocortone solution, again with marked improvement noted and the elimination of this pending complication.

Recheck on March 13, 1997, showed her to be using the hand freely for all types of activities and work duties. She was still bothered some with coldness of the hand compared to the opposite hand although circulation was definitely intact. Recommended hot soapy dishwater as well as other exercises and marked forcing of the hand in full activity usage and work. Recheck on April 15, 1997, showed patient with an additional complication of tenderness over the median nerve in the carpal tunnel of the volar wrist. This is a carpal tunnel syndrome, following the Colles' fracture, and is known to develop particularly in very communited severe types of Colles' fractures, occasionally. This was recognized, and treatment measures recommended for her along conservative lines. She failed to improve sufficiently with these measures and by September 21, 1997, the carpal tunnel syndrome, although improved, was still present and handicapping her. We injected the carpal tunnel on this date with Xylocaine and Hydrocortone solution to see if this would be helpful, and to see if surgery could be prevented. We last rechecked her on December 21, 1997, and the injection had been successful, clearing up the carpal tunnel syndrome. She was using the hand freely for everything at this time, had an excellent range of motion in the thumb and fingers, made a good tight fist, with good strength. The hand was normally warm. The Colles' fracture had excellent contours and good range of wrist motion present. She was finally dismissed at this time from medical care as having reached maximum medical recovery.

In summary, she sustained a rather severe type of fracture of the forearm and wrist, as detailed above, which was somewhat complicated by various complications in her case, which were fortunately recognized and properly and adequately treated with subsequent good response and result obtained. However, it is estimated that she has at least a 10% to 15% permanent partial disability rating in the hand and wrist as a permanent residual.

Sincerely yours,

Ralph D. Ellman, M.D., F.A.C.S., F.I.C.S.

D. NOTES AND QUESTIONS ON PLAINTIFF'S ATTORNEY'S INITIAL FILE

1. CASE ACCEPTANCE; UNDERTAKING OF ATTORNEY-CLIENT RELATIONSHIP. If you were an attorney in Mr. Elder's situation, would you have accepted employment in this case? (Hint: By this time, you may have been trained to think principally in terms of proof of a prima facie case against the defendant. What other kinds of matters should you consider, and how should they influence you?)

2. INTERVIEW OF THE PLAINTIFF. Plaintiff's attorney undertook a more thorough interview of the Plaintiff than the notes would indicate (these notes are a facsimile of those actually taken by Plaintiff's attorney, with only names and places changed). Many attorneys use data collection forms analogous to those used in the claim file, above, for the collection of standard information. Some types of practice (e.g., divorce, compensation, collection, and some types of personal injury work) lend themselves well to standardized data collection. Coordination of the use of a form with a free-flow interview is essential.

3. OFFICE SYSTEMS; DATES AND DEADLINES. Careful attorneys maintan a double-entry calendar system (that is, one in which two people, ususally the attorney and a secretary, separately enter upcoming dates), as well as a long-range calendar. What date should the Plaintiff's attorney enter immediately on his calendar in this case? (Hint: The statute of limitations for personal injury actions in West York is two years; the accident occurred on May 7, 1996; and the demand letter is dated January 27, 1998). Since a busy attorney may have responsibility for a hundred, or even several hundred, matters, all with shifting dates, scheduling is a factor of no small importance to the litigating lawyer.

4. DEMAND LETTER. The letter informing the defendant of one's demand is called a "demand letter." Should a good demand letter be conciliatory and disclose potential weaknesses in one's case, or should it be clear, direct and positive? Would you think it likely that settlement would ever result from a demand letter?

5. FEE AGREEMENT: PLAINTIFF'S ATTORNEY HAS FOLLOWED ONE OF THE CARDINAL RULES OF GOOD PRACTICE BY OBTAINING A WRITTEN FEE AGREEMENT. Many attorneys give great attention to the wording of the fee contract, because it establishes the relationship, takes care of financial matters, and prevents malpractice through misunderstandings. See, e.g., J. Foonberg, How to Start and Build a Law Practice (1978). Many insist on simple wording so the client can understand his obligations. It is worth taking care in drafting and filling blanks in the fee contract. For example, the definition of the claim is left blank in this case; what is the attorney's responsibility if plaintiff has a potential claim for (say) insurance proceeds arising from the same accident, and she loses it through non-assertion? Or if a counterclaim is filed? Inclusion of the following matters in the contract is typical: authorization to pay expenses on behalf of the client (such as the physician's fee); an explicit statement that such expenses are to be reimbursed by the client; a list of obligations of the client (such as appearing for deposition, furnishing information, telling the truth, and refraining from insistence upon illegal or unethical action); and an explicit statement that if nothing is recovered, nothing is owed (implicit-

ly stated, but clients appreciate having it made explicit); in addition to the matters covered by this contract.

6. MEDICAL AUTHORIZATION. Health care providers will not generally release information without patient authorization. It often happens that a client may have consulted with several physicians, and may give the attorney the name of the wrong one; in that event, how should the attorney obtain further authorizations—by mailing forms to the client, or by having the client come to the attorney's office? (Hint: This is a trick question. What the attorney actually did in this case—and what many attorneys do—is to obtain the client's signature on a number of authorizations at once, in blank).

7. EXTENT OF INVESTIGATION. The demand letter states, "my investigation" indicates that Scott's was negligent. How extensive an "investigation" is Plaintiff's attorney likely to have conducted thus far? Why? Notice that he has gone to the effort of acquiring fairly extensive information from the physician regarding Plaintiff's damage, which he evidently considers nearly as important as liability. It is customary to pay the physician a fee, on the order of $250 to $500, for this narrative statement, as it is called.

CHAPTER THREE:

PLEADINGS, DISCOVERY, AND INITIAL PRETRIAL PROCEEDINGS

A. SUMMONS, COMPLAINT, AND SERVICE

SUMMONS

United States District Court

FOR THE

MIDDLE DISTRICT OF WEST YORK, LONDON DIVISION

CA-71
CIVIL ACTION FILE No. 4683

MIRANDA DOMINGUEZ,

Plaintiff

v.

SCOTT'S FOOD STORES, INC.

Defendant

SUMMONS

To the above named Defendant :

You are hereby summoned and required to serve upon   Stephen T. Elder

plaintiff's attorney , whose address is First Savings Building, London, West York
77002,

an answer to the complaint which is herewith served upon you, within   20 . days after service of this

summons upon you, exclusive of the day of service. If you fail to do so, judgment by default will be

taken against you for the relief demanded in the complaint.

W.B. Lewis
——————————————
Clerk of Court.

Brenda Morgan
Brenda Morgan,   *Deputy Clerk.*

Date: February 19, 1998   [Seal of Court]

COMPLAINT

IN THE UNITED STATES DISTRICT COURT
FOR THE MIDDLE DISTRICT OF WEST YORK
LONDON DIVISION

MIRANDA DOMINGUEZ, Plaintiff   )
v.   )   NO. CA-71-4683
SCOTT'S FOOD STORES, INC., Defendant)

COMPLAINT

     Comes now Miranda Dominguez, hereinafter called Plaintiff,
complaining of Scott's Food Stores, Inc., hereinafter called
Defendant, and would respectfully show the Court as follows:

JURISDICTION, SERVICE AND VENUE

     1. Plaintiff is a citizen of the State of West York and
Defendant is a corporation incorporated under the laws of the
State of Texafornia, having its principal place of business in
a state other than the State of West York. The matter in contro-
versy exceeds, exclusive of interest and costs, the sum of
Seventy-five Thousand Dollars.

16

2. Defendant maintains, owns and operates a chain of food stores within the State of West York, from which it derives revenue. Such conduct constitutes "doing business" within the meaning of W.Y.Civ.Stat.Ann. art. 2031b (Vernon 1964) and supplies the minimum contacts necessary to support this Court's jurisdiction. The claims herein asserted arose out of the business done by Defendant in the State of West York, as required by art. 2031b.

3. All Plaintiffs reside in, and the claim or claims asserted herein arose in, the Middle District of West York, London Division. Further, the Defendant Corporation is doing business in such district and division.

CLAIM FOR NEGLIGENCE

4. This suit is brought for the recovery of the damages to which your Plaintiff is legally entitled as the result of an accident which occurred on or about May 7, 1996, at the Scott Food Store No. 14, located at 1100 Quitman, London, Manero County, West York.

5. At this time, Plaintiff was getting a shopping cart from a stacked row when she slipped and fell due to the improper manner in which the carts were aligned and the unsafe condition of Defendant's floor, causing injuries to Plaintiff.

6. Defendant and its agents failed to observe the applicable statutory laws and ordinances and failed to exercise that degree of care in the maintenance of their premises as would have been exercised by a person of ordinary prudence under the same or similar circumstances, all of which conduct constituted negligence. Such negligence was a proximate cause of Plaintiff's injuries.

7. Plaintiff has incurred physical pain, mental anguish, charges for medical services, lost household work, and lost enjoyment, as well as other damages, and she will in all probability incur further such damages in the future. Such damages exceed the value of $75,000.

CONCLUSION AND PRAYER

Wherefore, Plaintiff prays that she recover of Defendant her damages, and that she have and recover such other relief, in law or in equity, general or special, to which she may prove herself justly entitled.

Respectfully submitted,

Stephen T. Elder

Stephen T. Elder
Suite 412
First Savings Building
London, West York 77002
666-111
Attorney for Plaintiff

NOTE ON SERVICE AND RETURN

Rule 10(b) of the Local Rules of the Middle District of West York supplements the service provisions of Rule 4, Fed. R. Civ. P.

The Local Rule provides: "Service of civil process shall not be executed by the United States marshal except for government initiated proceedings, in forma pauperis process, extraordinary writs or when ordered to do so by a judge." The rule is an effort to allocate expenses to private litigants rather than to the government and to promote efficiency, in that litigants sometimes know better than the marshal how to find defendants with whom they have had dealings.

The rule further provides that plaintiff's attorney "will be responsible for designating a person over the age of 18 years who is not a party or attorney in the case, to make service." The service may be made either in the form of "personal service pursuant to Rule 4(d)(1)-(7), Fed. R. Civ. P." or by "mailing a copy of the pleadings and summons" pursuant to Rule 4(d)(8) to the defendant by registered or certified mail, return receipt requested, "with delivery restricted to addressee only." The Local Rule also provides that service on the West York Secretary of State pursuant to the West York long-arm statute may be accomplished either by personal service on the Secretary or by certified mail. This service is consistent with Rule 4(e), which provides for use of the long-arm statute of the State in which the district court is located, and with the West York long-arm statute, which requires the Secretary to forward the process to defendant's last-known address by registered or certified mail restricted to the addressee. The Local Rule provides for the requisite number of copies and for a check to be submitted to the Secretary for a written "certification" that the service has, or has not, been effected.

Pursuant to this rule, Elder designated his own secretary (who was not a party or attorney) as process server, and she sent the preceding documents by restricted certified mail together with an explanatory cover letter (which Elder dictated) and a check for $12.00. Upon receipt from the West York Secretary of State of a certificate, in standard form and with a beautifully embossed gold seal, confirming that the service had been accomplished, the mailing made, and the return receipt received with an endorsement from the addressee, Elder filed the certificate along with the following return, which was sworn to by his secretary as process server.

RETURN ON SERVICE OF WRIT

I hereby certify and return that on the ___19th___ day of ___February___ , 1998 ,

I received this summons and served it together with the complaint herein as follows:
by serving same upon the Secretary of State of the State of West York, by mail, as the agent of defendant, and by his mailing same, return receipt requested, to defendant, and certifying receipt by the attached certificate
(For service made by mail:

I hereby certify that I mailed this summons on ___February 19,___ , 19 98 ,

at ___London, West York___ ; and that such service was
place of mailing

☒ accepted   ☐ refused   ☐ returned but not refused.

B. DEFENDANT'S ATTACK ON THE COMPLAINT

DEFENDANT'S RULE 12 MOTION

IN THE UNITED STATES DISTRICT COURT
FOR THE MIDDLE DISTRICT OF WEST YORK
LONDON DIVISION

MIRANDA DOMINGUEZ, Plaintiff   )
v.   )   NO. CA-71-4683
SCOTT'S FOOD STORES, INC., Defendant)

MOTION TO DISMISS, TO STRIKE,
OR FOR MORE DEFINITE STATEMENT

Comes now Scott's Food Stores, Inc., Defendant in the above styled and numbered cause, and moves the court as follows:

1. To dismiss the action pursuant to Rule 12(b)(6) because the complaint fails to state a claim against Defendant upon which relief can be granted.

2. To strike from the complaint, pursuant to Rule 12(f), that portion of paragraph 6 alleging that Defendant or its agents failed "to observe the applicable statutory laws and ordinances", because the allegation fails to give notice of any statutory laws or ordinances allegedly violated, and it is therefore insufficient.

3. To order a more definite statement pursuant to Rule 12(e). As required in that Rule, Defendant hereby points out the defects complained of and the details desired:

    a. That portion of paragraph 6 alleging that Defendant or its agents failed "to observe the applicable statutory laws and ordinances" is insufficient to give Defendant notice, and Defendant desires details giving notice of the statutory laws or ordinances allegedly violated, if any.

    b. That portion of paragraph 5 alleging that Plaintiff slipped and fell "due to the improper manner in which the carts were aligned and the unsafe condition of Defendant's floor" is insufficient to give Defendant notice of the manner in which the cart alignment was improper or the manner in which the condition of Defendant's floor was unsafe or the manner in which Scott's Food Stores, Inc. was negligent. Defendant desires details showing in what manner the alignment was improper or the floor unsafe.

Wherefore, Defendant prays that the Court dismiss the action, or, in the alternative, that it strike the portion of paragraph 6 identified herein, or, in the alternative, that it grant the more definite statement prayed for.

Respectfully submitted,

Robert L. Livingston, Jr.

McIntosh & Walker
by Robert L. Livingston, Jr.
First City National Bank Bldg.
London, West York 77002

C. NOTES AND QUESTIONS ON INITIAL PLEADINGS AND ORDER

1. CLIENT RELATIONS. Immediately after receiving the case and filing an answer, Mr. Livingston would normally write a letter to his client, acknowledging having been retained and having received the file, giving a brief and cautious evaluation of the case (in this instance, he evaluated the case on liability as not a strong one, but having the potential of being submitted to a jury, and with substantial medical expense for the type of injury), and telling his client what was ahead (challenges to the pleadings, depositions, etc.).

Realizing that he was in a service business, Mr. Livingston also advised his client in his letter that he welcomed inquiries and would send progress reports. Some attorneys (including Livingston) set aside a time each day of two hours or so for telephone inquiries; Livingston's letter advised of the best time to reach him. Even if the client was one of long standing, as was Scott's Foods here, the letter could be expected to contain assurances that the matter would receive prompt attention and thanks for the client's confidence. Many attorneys in this situation also send copies of materials generated by the proceedings (e.g., the pleadings) so that the client can see for itself what is being done. Without this practice, many clients do not appreciate, and indeed cannot be expected to understand, a bill for unseen services.

2. THE COMPLAINT: JURISDICTION AND VENUE. What are the elements of subject-matter jurisdiction? Does the complaint supply them? As for in personam jurisdiction, why does the complaint refer to, and allege compliance with, a West York statute, since this is a complaint filed in federal court? Is the venue proper? If so, why?

3. THE COMPLAINT: SUFFICIENCY AND SPECIFICITY. What is the standard for substantive sufficiency of the complaint to state a claim? Does this complaint meet that standard? What degree of specificity is required, and does this complaint meet it? (Hint: Compare it to the forms appended to the Federal Rules, particularly Form 9, entitled "complaint for negligence.")

4. DRAFTING OF DEFENDANT'S MOTIONS. Can defendant realistically expect dismissal, and if not, can it move for dismissal in good faith? In terms of tactics, why has defendant moved for all three types of relief—to dismiss, to strike, and for more definite statement—rather than choosing the most likely type of relief (e.g., more definite statement) and moving for it alone?

5. DOES THE MOTION TO DISMISS COMPLY WITH RULE 11, THE REASONABLENESS-IN-PLEADINGS RULE? Rule 11 requires that all pleadings be supportable by arguments of law and fact based on a "reasonable investigation." If a lawyer cant keep a straight face in arguing in favor of a motion, it violates Rule 11, and perhaps that is the case here. Doesn't it seem that the motion to dismiss violates this rule?

6. TACTICS AS TO SPECIFICITY. Plaintiff has intentionally pled the complaint quite broadly. Defendant's lawyer wants the court to force plaintiff to plead with more specificity. In terms of tactics, why? (Hint: Many students recognize that defendant wants to find out about plaintiff's claim, but that can be done through discovery. The complaint sets the outer parameters of the proof that can support recovery; does this function of pleadings explain why the defense lawyer wants more specificity?)

7. DRAFTING OF THE PROPOSED ORDER. Defendant drafted a proposed order for the court and attached it to the motion. While it may seem strange for a party to draft an order for the court to enter, such an approach may be tactically wise and may be required by custom or local rule. Of course, the court is not obligated to enter the proposed order.

8. COURT'S RULING ON THE MOTION. Courts vary widely in the manner in which they schedule, hear, and consider motions. Under the local rules of the Middle District of West York, a "submission date" is fixed by the parties if they can agree on one, and by the court if not. After that date, the court may rule on the motion without further argument. Unless the parties request argument, and the court grants it, or unless the motion requires the taking of evidence, the court determines the motion on the basis of the written submissions alone. In this case, the court adopted the proposed order, deleting the inappropriate words.

```
                IN THE UNITED STATES DISTRICT COURT
                FOR THE MIDDLE DISTRICT OF WEST YORK
                           LONDON DIVISION


MIRANDA DOMINGUEZ, Plaintiff          )
v.                                    )    NO. CA-71-4683
SCOTT'S FOOD STORE, INC., Defendant   )


                  ORDER ON DEFENDANT'S MOTIONS

        Came on this day to be heard Defendant's Motion to Dismiss,
   to Strike, or for More Definite Statement, and the court, after
   considering the Pleadings and the arguments of counsel, is of the
   opinion that they should be determined as follows, and it is
   therefore
        ORDERED, ADJUDGED AND DECREED that Defendant's motion to
   dismiss is hereby granted/denied; and
           that Defendant's motion to strike is granted/denied; and
           that Defendant's motion for more definite statement is granted/
   denied; and
           that Plaintiff is ordered to file an amended complaint within
   90        days.
        Signed and entered on March 25, 1998.

                              John T. Hughes
                          United States District Judge
```

D. EARLY CONFERENCE AND SETTLEMENT EFFORTS

INITIAL PRETRIAL CONFERENCE

[Using a standard form of pretrial setting notice, the court ordered both attorneys to appear on April 2, 1998, in the court's chambers. Attorneys Elder and Livingston appeared. The conference was held not in the courtroom, but around a conference table in the judge's office. Once the parties had greeted each other, the following ensued:]

THE COURT: Well, I tell you, gentlemen, I almost got rid of my crystal ball last weekend, when the Dallas Cowboys beat the West York Tigers. I could have sworn those Tigers were going to the Super Bowl this year.

But I'll tell you what. I don't have my crystal ball any more, but I don't need a crystal ball to tell you what really ought to happen to this case. It really ought to be settled. And both of you know that it ought to be settled.

Bob, have you made him an offer? I don't want to know what it is, you understand, but I just want to know whether you've given your best shot to settling this case.

LIVINGSTON: Judge, we've made them an offer, and I think it's a great deal more than the case is worth. I can tell you quite earnestly that we think that it's top dollar.

From our standpoint, you've got to keep this in mind: The lady had a case before. She fell in a Scott's Food Store, and we settled that claim with her. We settled that one even though there wasn't liability, in our opinion, and we settled it for more than we thought it was worth. There comes a point when we have to sort of put our foot down, and when we don't have any liability, and the complaint doesn't tell us anything, we just can't go beyond the amount that we've already offered in this case.

THE COURT: Now, have you <turning to Plaintiff's attorney> visited with your client about what they've offered?

ELDER: Yes, but here's the situation: They made the lady a settlement offer before I represented her. When she came into my office, I advised her not to accept it. It doesn't begin to compensate her for the injury she's got and will have for the rest of her life. In good conscience, I can't recommend it to her.

THE COURT: Well, you need to consider the fact that this is a slip-and-fall case, and of course I don't know the exact facts of your case and. I make no prejudgment, but it's awful hard to establish liability in this type of case. You can't get by with just proving that your client fell in a Scott's Food Store. In fact, you can't even get by by showing that there was some sort of dangerous condition, unless you can show that Scott's was responsible for creating that dangerous condition and that it was unreasonable.

I always remember a case that I call the "Grape" case. It's a West York case, I forget the style. A lady went into a grocery store and slipped on a grape. But she couldn't prove that the store put the grape on the floor, or allowed it to get on the floor, or ignored it on the floor for an unreasonable length of time, and so she didn't recovery anything. That's the law.

LIVINGSTON: That's correct, Judge, and that's the type of situation we have here.

THE COURT: Well, anyway, have you made a counteroffer to them? And have you given it your best shot?

ELDER: Yes, your honor, I have. I feel most cases can be settled, and I try to settle every one, and I've tried with this one.

THE COURT: Well, all right. I'm going to see whether I can get you off the dime. How much discovery do you think you're going to need?

LIVINGSTON: Well, we'd like to start out by taking the Plaintiff's deposition. That's the only one I know of that we would want to take. There might be other discovery that we need to do, depending on what we find out.

THE COURT: I understand. I'm going to enter an order, then, requiring that discovery be completed by the end of this summer, August 31, and that the parties file a proposed pretrial order on or before September 30.

[The judge then wrote a handwritten memorandum, from which a short pretrial order called a "Docket Control Order" was prepared and entered, containing the discovery and pretrial timetables mentioned above.]

ORDER RESULTING FROM PRETRIAL CONFERENCE

IN THE UNITED STATES DISTRICT COURT
FOR THE MIDDLE DISTRICT OF WEST YORK
LONDON DIVISION

DOMINGUEZ   §
VS.   §   CIVIL ACTION NO. CA-71-4683
SCOTT'S FOOD STORES, INC.   §

DOCKET CONTROL ORDER

The following schedule will be adhered to. All communications concerning the case will be directed to George Davis, Courtroom Deputy, P.O. Box 303, London, West York 77002, (222) 321-2323.

1. _Not applicable_ NEW PARTIES WILL BE JOINED BY THIS DATE. The Attorney causing such joinder will provide copies of this Docket Control Order to the new parties.

2. _August 31, 1998_ DISCOVERY WILL BE COMPLETED BY THIS DATE.

3. _September 30, 1998_ MOTION CUT-OFF DATE. No motion will be considered after this date except for good cause shown. See Local Rule 15.

4. _September 30, 1998_ A JOINT PRETRIAL ORDER will be filed on or before this date. COUNSEL FOR PLAINTIFF IS RESPONSIBLE FOR THE TIMELY FILING OF THE JOINT PRETRIAL ORDER. All counsel are responsible for complying with all requirements of the Joint Pretrial Order. See Local Rules Appendix D-1.

DATE: _April 2, 1998_   _John T. Hughes_
                                             JOHN T. HUGHES
READ AND UNDERSTOOD: UNITED STATES DISTRICT JUDGE
Stephen T. Elder
Robert S. Livingston Jr.

E. DISCOVERY

PLAINTIFF'S REQUEST FOR ADMISSIONS AND DEFENDANT'S ANSWERS

IN THE UNITED STATES DISTRICT COURT
FOR THE MIDDLE DISTRICT OF WEST YORK
LONDON DIVISION

MIRANDA DOMINGUEZ, Plaintiff)
v.) NO. CA-71-4683
SCOTT'S FOOD STORES, INC., Defendant)

PLAINTIFF'S REQUEST FOR ADMISSIONS FROM DEFENDANT

In accordance with Rule 36, Federal Rules of Civil Procedure, Plaintiff requests that Defendant admit, for purposes of the pending action only, the truth of the matters herein set forth. You are instructed that a matter set forth herein is admitted unless, within 30 days after service of the request, Defendant serves upon Plaintiff a written answer or objection addressed to such matter, signed by Defendant or its attorney. In accordance with Rule 37, Federal Rules of Civil Procedure, you are notified that, if Defendant fails to admit the truth of any matter requested hereunder, and if Plaintiff thereafter proves the truth of such matter, Plaintiff will apply to the Court for an order requiring Defendant to pay the reasonable expenses incurred in making such proof, including reasonable attorney's fees. The matters as to which admissions are sought are as follows:

1. That defendant, on May 7, 1996, owned, maintained, and operated a store on Quitman Street in London, Manero County, West York.

Response: *Admitted.*

2. That on May 7, 1996, personnel operating Scott's Food Store No. 14 in London, Manero County, West York, were employed by defendant.

Response: *Admitted.*

3. That, on May 7, 1996, at Scott's Food Store No. 14, Defendant furnished shopping carts or baskets for the use of customers.

Response: *Admitted.*

4. That when, on or about May 7, 1996, Plaintiff attempted to obtain a shopping basket for use in Scott's Food Store No. 14 in London, Manero County, West York, Defendant was legally responsible for the condition of such carts.

Response: *Denied. Defendant must qualify its response by stating that it owned and maintained the carts in question, but because plaintiff has furnished no information concerning what, if any, condition allegedly caused the incident in dispute here, defendant has no information upon which to determine the responsibility of any person or party for such condition, and therefore must deny such responsibility.*

Respectfully submitted,

Stephen T. Elder
Stephen T. Elder
Suite 412,
First Savings Building
711 Fannin Street
London, West York   77002
666-1111
Attorney for Plaintiff

[An officer of defendant verified (i.e., swore under oath to) the answers. The verification is omitted here.]

24

NOTE ON AGREEMENT FOR DEPOSITION SCHEDULE

In early April of 1998, Mr. Livingston and Mr. Elder agreed by telephone at Mr. Livingston's request to a date for the taking of Ms. Dominguez' deposition. As a result of that conversation, Mr. Livingston sent the following letter confirming the deposition schedule:

"Dear Steve:

"This will confirm our agreement to take Mrs. Dominguez' deposition in your office at 3:00 p.m. on May 6, 1998.

"I will furnish the court reporter."

Mr. Elder, by letter, replied: "I will see you on the 6th."

DEPOSITION OF PLAINTIFF

IN THE UNITED STATES DISTRICT COURT
FOR THE MIDDLE DISTRICT OF WEST YORK,
LONDON DIVISION

MIRANDA DOMINGUEZ   )
V.   ) No. CA-71-4683
SCOTT'S FOOD STORES, INC.)

On the 6th day of May, 1998, at the offices of Stephen T. Elder, 301 First Savings Building, London, Manero County, West York, Miranda Dominguez appeared before me, Dan R. Curtis, a notary public of Manero County, West York, and being by me first duly sworn, testified by her oral deposition as hereinafter set out, pursuant to agreement of counsel for the respective parties that:

All formalities precedent to and incident to the taking and return of the deposition were waived; without making any objection at the time of taking, either party to the suit should have right at the time of trial to urge objections to questions or answers appearing in the deposition; and

The deposition might be filed in court unsigned, the signature of the witness being waived.

EXAMINATION BY MR. LIVINGSTON:

Q   Would you state your full name, please, ma'am?
A   Miranda Dominguez.
Q   How old a lady are you, Ms. Dominguez?
A   60 right now.
Q   Ms. Dominguez, my name is Robert Livingston, and I represent Scott's Food Stores in this suit that you filed against them. Do you understand that?
A   Yes, sir.
Q   I am going to ask you some questions. If you don't understand any question, please stop me and I'll be happy to repeat it. If you do understand my question, I'll expect you to go ahead and answer it accordingly. Has your attorney explained to you what a deposition is?
A   Yes.

Q   You understand that testimony that you give here today is subject to the same pains and penalties for perjury as if you were testifying in a court of law before a judge and jury; do you understand that?

A   Yes, sir.

Q   Where do you presently live, Ms. Dominguez?

A   2944 Dunham.

Q   Okay. How long have you lived at that address, Ms. Dominguez?

A   A year.

Q   Where did you live before that?

A   304 Southmore.

Q   Is that in London?

A   Yes, sir.

Q   How many children do you have?

A   One daughter.

Q   What is your husband's name?

A   Edward.

Q   How long have you been married to Edward Dominguez?

A   27 years.

Q   Is this your only marriage?

A   Yes, sir.

Q   How much education do you have?

A   I went through junior school.

Q   Are you presently employed?

A   No, sir.

Q   When was the last time that you were employed?

A   '46.

Q   What have you been doing since 1946? Have you been a housewife?

A   That's right.

Q   What is your daughter's name?

A   Thelma Rodriguez.

Q   Does she live here in London?

A   Yes, sir.

Q   Have you ever had your deposition taken before?

A   No, sir.

Q   Have you ever make any claim against anyone for any sort of injures or anything of this nature before this claim?

A   Yes, I did one time.

Q   Tell me about that, please.

A   That was when I hurt my leg.

Q   Where did you hurt your leg?

A   In Scott's, the same store.

Q   When was that?

A   I don't remember what year it was. It's been a long time.

Q   Did you file a lawsuit?

A   Yes, sir.

Q   Was the case tried or settled?

A   It was settled in the lawyer's office.

Q   Was it 10 years ago or more?

A   It's more than 10 years.

Q   On what date did this present accident happen?

A   On May 7th, 1996.

Q   Have you ever made claim against anyone other than Scott's?

A   No, sir.

Q   What day of the week was May 7th, 1996?

A   It was a Thursday.

Q   Why were you in the store?

A   I was doing -- going to do our shopping.

Q   Tell me what happened.

A   I walked in the store, and I was going to get my basket. And they was all stuck together. And I pulled with my right hand and they were all, at the beginning --

Q   In other words, they were inside each other, like they stack them?

A   Yes. And I pulled with my right hand. Here come three or four baskets and they pushed me down. And I put my right hand on the floor to think to keep from falling down, and that was when I broke my hand.

Q   Let me back up for just a minute and run through this piece by piece here. You came into the store and you went through the turnstile, didn't you?

A   Yes, sir.

Q   And you went over to where they stack the baskets?

A   That's right.

Q   And these baskets are stuck one inside each other, they stack them?

A   Uh-huh.

Q   And you reached over with your hand?

A   With my right hand.

Q   Right hand. To pull the basket loose?

A   Yes, sir.

Q   And about three or four baskets came out, and the basket ran over you and you lost your balance, it that right?

A   That's right, yes.

Q   And you fell down, and when you landed, you landed --

A   On my right hand.

Q   -- on your right hand?

A   The first thing I know, my hand was turned backwards and was all purple and I was just in pain. I couldn't stand it! I went through a lot of pain.

Q   Do you know why the baskets stuck together?

A   Sir?

Q   Do you know why the baskets stuck together?

A   No. In the beginning they have all baskets there, sir.

Q   They always stack them in the same way inside each other?

A   Yes.

Q   And you have shopped in that store every week, haven't you?

A   Yes.

Q   And every week when you go in there, the baskets are stacked in the same way?

A   Yes, sir.

Q   And this was no different; they were stacked in the same way, inside each other?

A   But they were too tight. And I just lost my balance and the baskets came toward my body.

Q   The only difference between this time and any other time that you'd been in the store and getting a basket was when you pulled this time about two or three or four baskets came out instead of just one, isn't that right?

A   Yes, sir.

Q   That's the only difference?

A   Yes.

Q   And you don't have any idea why the two or three or four of them stayed together?

A   No, sir.

Q   Was there anything else that caused you to fall other than these baskets?

A   It had rained that day, and the floor was kind of damp and that was what made me fall down, too.

Q   The floor was wet?

A   Yes. Kind of damp. Not exactly wet, but damp, people going in and out.

Q   People were walking in and out and it was raining that day?
A   It wasn't raining when I went in, but it had rained that day.
Q   You testified, I believe, that these baskets kind of made you lose your balance and you fell because the baskets made you lose your balance?
A   Yes.
Q   Did your feet slip?
A   No. I slipped after the basket pushed me down.
Q   So, then, the water on the floor really didn't cause you to fall; the baskets caused you to fall?
A   Yes, you can say the baskets.
Q   And you have already testified, Ms. Dominguez, that you didn't slip, that you lost your balance when you pulled these baskets out and about three or four baskets came out at you?
A   Yes.
Q   And that is what caused you to fall and land on the floor?
A   Yes.
Q   You said that the floor was kind of damp?
A   Yes, sir.
Q   Can you describe it any more than "just kind of damp"?
A   No. Just kind of damp. That's all I can tell you.
Q   You didn't look at the floor to determine whether it was dirty or clean or anything like that?
A   No. I was concerned about my hand, that's all, my hand, the way it was.
Q   Did you ever make any sort of inspection of the baskets?
A   No, sir.
Q   Were you taken to the doctor?
A   Dr. Ellman at County Memorial Hospital.
Q   Had you been to Dr. Ellman before?
A   Yes, sir.
Q   When had you been to Dr. Ellman before?
A   When I had that fall.
Q   Who sent you to Dr. Ellman?
A   I went on my own.
Q   Who recommended Dr. Ellman when you had that fall?
A   A friend of mine.
Q   All right. Who is the friend?
A   I couldn't remember, sir.
Q   It was not your lawyer?
A   No, sir.

[At this point, Mr. Livingston asked a number of questions as to when the witness saw Dr. Ellman, when he released her, how often she went to see him, what hospitals she was in, and the like. The witness' testimony, in substance, was that she went every week during the first month after the accident; then the doctor removed the cast; and, finding her arm swelling, he put her in the hospital for two weeks, at County Memorial Hospital. Thereafter, she continued to see the doctor every "two months or every three weeks," as Ms. Dominguez puts it. She ceased to see Dr. Ellman when he released her. The witness states, "I can't remember" whether the release date was one year ago or three.]

Q   Do you know how much your medical bills have been?
A   Yes. I got them over here in my purse, the bills.
Q   Will you look at them and see how much they are?
A   Dr. Ellman is 285 and Dr. Bowers is $96.00.

Q   That was the x-ray doctor or the anesthesiologist?
A   The one that give me some kind of shot in my arm to get the swelling out.
      And the hospital, my insurance paid some, and the balance is $696.30.
Q   Do you know how much your insurance paid?
A   Sir?
Q   Do you know how much your insurance paid?
A   85 -- $89.25. That was all my insurance paid.
Q   So, your total hospital bill was in the amount of about $785?
A   Yes. And the balance is $696.30. And then for the first night I went in
      the hospital it was $95.25 when I broke my hand. Dr. Ellman kept me that
      night overnight in the hospital.
Q   Did your insurance pay any portion of Dr. Ellman's bill?
A   A hundred.
Q   The 285 you gave me, is that the balance?
A   That's the balance.
Q   Is this all of your bills?
A   That's right.
Q   And you have any other out-of-pocket expenses other than Dr. Ellman's and
      Dr. Bowers' and those hospital bills?
A   No. Except my husband taking a lot of days off to take me to the doctor.
      He used to take off from work and didn't get no pay.

[Here, Mr. Livingston asked questions to pin down the employment and wage rate of the witness' husband. The witness stated that her husband worked at Williams Floor Company and earned $ 3.25 per hour. He is a floor finisher. When she went to the hospital, the witness testified, her husband would lose a day's work and wages.]

Q   And you haven't seen any doctors other than Dr. Bowers and Dr. Ellman?
A   No, sir.
Q   You were speaking a moment ago of dampness on the floor. Do you know how
      long this dampness had been on the floor?

[Here Mr. Livingston established that the dampness was caused by people walking around with wet shoes; that the witness herself walked outside where it was wet before coming in, though "not too much;" that the witness would "drag some of this wetness in, would't you?" "Yes, sir;" and that the witness had no idea how long the dampness had been there and did not know how it would have gotten there other than by customers tracking it in.]

Q   But, Ms. Dominguez, as I understand your testimony, you did not slip; you
      lost your balance because of these buggies; isn't that right?
A   Yes, sir.
Q   So this damp floor didn't have anything to do with your falling, did it?
A   No.
Q   Was anyone with you in the store that day?
A   No, I went in by myself.
Q   Have you ever seen customers putting baskets in and taking baskets out of the
      area where the baskets are kept?
A   Well, I haven't noticed that.
Q   You haven't noticed that?
A   No, sir.
Q   They could; you just haven't noticed it; is that correct?
A   Well, I don't know.

Q   Now, is it your testimony that you pulled the basket with your right hand and then placed your right hand down and it broke it?
A   Yes, sir.
Q   You didn't pull the baskets with your left hand?
A   No. I pulled it with my right hand.
Q   Were you looking at the baskets when you pulled them?
A   Yes, sir, I was.
Q   Were you stopped?
A   Yes, sir.
Q   Was there anyone else around you that came up to you and tried to help you?
A   No, sir, there was nobody there.
Q   There was nobody in the immediate area that saw the fall?
A   No, sir, I don't think so. I didn't see anybody there, sir.
Q   And I believe you have already testified you don't know what caused the buggies to stick together?
A   Well, you can put it that way.
Q   Do you know what caused them to stick together?
A   Well, they were just all stuck together, that's all I can explain to you.
Q   In other words, you don't know why they were stuck together?
A   No, sir.
Q   They were just stuck together?
A   Yes.
Q   And three or four of them came out when you pulled?
A   That's right.
Q   You didn't see them tied together or anything like that?
A   No, I didn't see whether they were tied or what, sir.

[Here Mr. Livingston asked whether the witness had "ever had any trouble with the police" ("No, sir"); had a social security number (she did, but she did not have the card with her or know the number); had a driver's license ("No"); had any hobbies, before or after the accident ("No, sir"); know how much time her husband had missed from work taking her to the doctor ("No, sir"); and, finally, whether she had understood his questions ("Yes, sir").]

MR LIVINGSTON: I don't have anything further.

EXAMINATION BY MR. ELDER:

Q   Ms. Dominguez, what is the main use of those carts that you were talking about?
A   You mean those wagons?
Q   Yes.
A   Well, they were all kind of stuck up together.
Q   No. No. No. What's the main use of them, the main function you saw them being put to in the store?
A   Well, sometimes the people leave them outside.
Q   But the primary function -- did you ever see them taken outside?
A   Yes. Some of the kids take them outside and play with them.
Q   Did you ever see anyone abandon a cart out there and leave it out in the parking lot?
A   I see a lot of people.
Q   Did you ever see these grocery baskets anywhere else in the neighborhood?
A   Yes. Around the neighborhood. Over there in January there was wagons all over the street down there. Especially on weekends. The kids would be playing with them up and down the street.

30

Q   What sort of games would they play with them?
A   Running them up and down the street.
Q   Did they ever run them into each other?
A   Yes.
Q   How long had you and your family been shopping there?
A   About 10 or 11 years.
Q   During that 10 or 11 years, had they used the same carts?
A   Yes, sir.
Q   Did you ever notice that the carts were bent?
A   Sometimes. I didn't pay any attention.
Q   Did you ever notice the carts were in less than perfect condition?
A   Yes, because the wheel would go this way and that way, wouldn't go straight.
Q   So, it would be fair to say that the carts were pretty old and rundown?
A   That's right.
Q   And in all that time, Ms. Dominguez, did you ever know Scott's to replace any of the carts?
A   Not in that store.
Q   Did you ever know them to repair any of the carts?
A   No, sir.
Q   Had you ever before had them to break loose in a whole row like this time when three or four carts came loose at once? Had that ever happened to you before?
A   No, sir, that's the first time it ever happened to me like that.

MR. ELDER: That's all.

EXAMINATION BY MR. LIVINGSTON:

Q   Ms. Dominguez, you never saw Scott's repairing the carts; this is your testimony?
A   Yes. Not in that store.
Q   You wouldn't know whether they repaired them or not, would you?
A   No, sir.

MR. LIVINGSTON: I don't have anything further.
[END OF DEPOSITION. The reporter's transcription reflects the waiver of signature at the end. On the final page is the reporter's certificate that the transcript was dictated and transcribed from his shorthand under his supervision and is a correct record of the proceedings.]

F. NOTES AND QUESTIONS ON DISCOVERY

1. USE OF DISCOVERY TO ENSURE THAT PLAINTIFF HAS SUED THE RIGHT DEFENDANT. Would you suspect that plaintiffs are frequently or infrequently concerned about having sued the wrong defendant? (Hint: What would be the result if Scott's Food Stores, Inc. simply licenses its trade name, without control, to a separate entity that operates Scott's Food Store No. 14—and the limitation period runs before plaintiff so discovers?)

2. DRAFTING AND USE OF WRITTEN DISCOVERY. Drafting and use of interrogatories and requests for admissions is an art form. If the propositions are too narrow, the likelihood increases that the response may be technically correct but misleading (example: "Does defendant have any photographs of the accident scene?" Defendant has a carefully prepared scale drawing that reproduces the scene as

definitively as a photograph, but answers, accurately, "No"). If the proposition is too broad, the response may be equally misleading, or it may be meaningless (Example: "Describe the accident." Answer: "I was injured due to defendant's negligence.") It can be expected that the responses to written discovery will be controlled by the opposing attorney, who will respond according to his own strategy. Note that plaintiff's attorney has here used four differently worded requests to establish the relatively simple proposition that he has sued the right defendant; note also that defendant has considered strategy in responding, but has been forthright (a phenomenon that is not universal.)

3. SETTING UP THE DEPOSITION; NOTICE. Fed R. Civ. P. 30 provides for notice of taking depositions, and Rule 45 provides for subpoena of non-parties. However, when there is a single plaintiff and a single defendant, and the attorneys find that they can cooperate, it is typical for discovery to be set up by an agreement reflected in an exchange of letters, as was done here. See Fed. R. Civ. P. 29 (authorizing such agreements). Indeed, it is impolite to pick a day without consulting the adversary, and it may result in conflicts making compliance impossible.

4. COVERAGE OF THE DEPOSITION. Defendant's attorney wants to find out about plaintiff's case, as thoroughly as he can, in both its favorable and its unfavorable aspects, and he wants to "freeze" the testimony in sworn form. If plaintiff deviates from the deposition at trial, it can be used to impeach her testimony. The deposition contains the following basic parts: initial assurance that plaintiff understands what the deposition is about (to enhance the impeachment function); the plaintiff's background and history; the incident itself, including relevant preceding and following events; and coverage of the various possible elements of damages.

5. DEPOSITION QUESTIONING TECHNIQUES. At trial, one would examine an adverse witness with narrow questions. It would be inadvisable, at trial, to ask such a question as, "What happened?" allowing the witness to tell his or her story. But notice the technique used by the defendant's attorney in this deposition: he begins by asking about the accident by asking, "Tell me what happened." Why? Initiation of questioning with a broad, open-ended inquiry encourages the witness to narrate. The result is fuller discovery than would result from specific questions formulated on the attorney's own limited knowledge of the incident. Continued narration should be encouraged by prompting, until the narrative potential of the witness is exhausted; only then should the attorney shift to more specific questions. This approach is sometimes called the "funnel" sequence (or "T-funnelling"), and although it is not appropriate for cross examination of an adverse witness at trial, it is useful both for discovery and for interviewing. Notice that defendant's attorney interrupted plaintiff's narrative shortly after he got her started talking; did he become impatient and deviate from the funnel sequence too early? Sometimes that is necessary, to finish the deposition in a reasonable time.

Note also the technique of leaving a subject and returning to it (as defendant's attorney does with respect to the "wet floor" allegations). What effect does the deposition have upon the claim that an "unsafe floor" contributed to plaintiff's injuries?

6. WHOM TO DEPOSE. Usually, only adverse witnesses are deposed (or those that are unlikely to be available for trial). If the witness is amenable to being interviewed in one's own office, there is usually no point in furnishing the questions and answers, under oath, to the adversary. In this case, however, plaintiff's attorney did take the unusual step of asking his client a few short questions. Why? (Hint: Without plaintiff's responses to these questions, might the state of the record have been such as to justify the filing of a motion for summary judgment by defendant?) Also, note that little deposition discovery (or other discovery, for that matter) was undertaken by either side in this case, as a result of economic considerations.

AMENDED COMPLAINT

IN THE UNITED STATES DISTRICT COURT
FOR THE MIDDLE DISTRICT OF WEST YORK
LONDON DIVISION

MIRANDA DOMINGUEZ, Plaintiff   )
v.   )   NO. CA-71-4683
SCOTT'S FOOD STORES, INC., Defendant)

AMENDED COMPLAINT

Comes now Miranda Dominguez, hereinafter called Plaintiff, complaining of Scott's Food Stores, Inc., hereinafter called Defendant, and would respectfully show the Court as follows:

JURISDICTION, SERVICE AND VENUE

1. Plaintiff is a citizen of the State of West York and Defendant is a corporation incorporated under the laws of the State of Texafornia, having its principal place of business in a state other than the State of West York. The matter in controversy exceeds, exclusive of interest and costs, the sum of Seventy-five Thousand Dollars.

2. Defendant has been served with process and has appeared. This court has jurisdiction of Defendant's person and venue is proper.

CLAIM FOR NEGLIGENCE

3. This suit is brought for the recovery of the damages to which your Plaintiff is legally entitled as the result of an accident which occurred on or about May 7, 1996, at the Scott Food Store No. 14, located at 1100 Quitman, London, Manero County, West York.

4. At that time, Mrs. Dominguez had just come into the store to shop for groceries. To carry her groceries, she sought to get a shopping cart from a row of carts stacked with the baskets inside each other as is customarily done in grocery stores.

5. The carts were in a bad state of repair: The baskets were bent, some of the wheels would not turn, and the tubular metal frames of some of the carts were bent.

6. In spite of the state of repair of the carts, Mrs. Dominguez had previously been able to pull one cart away from the rack without difficulty.

7. On the occasion in question, three or four baskets stuck together, and all started rolling toward Mrs. Dominguez. The baskets ran over Mrs. Dominguez. She was knocked off balance and fell to the floor.

8. The baskets in question were owned and maintained by Defendant and were furnished by it for the use of customers.

9. Defendant and its agents failed to exercise that degree of care in the maintenance of their store as would have been exercised by a person of ordinary prudence under the same or similar circumstances. Specifically, Defendant and its employees at Store No. 14 ought not to have crammed the bent and broken carts together, or ought to have made sure that they were in sufficiently good repair that an elderly lady could pull a single cart away from a row. Such failure constituted negligence, which was a proximate cause of plaintiff's injuries.

10. Plaintiff has incurred physical pain, mental anguish, charges for medical services, lost household work, and lost enjoyment, as well as other damages, and she will in all probability incur further such damages in the future. Such damages exceed the value of $75,000.

CONCLUSION AND PRAYER

Wherefore, Plaintiff prays that she recover of Defendant her damages, and that she have and recover such other relief, in law or in equity, general or special, to which she may prove herself justly entitled.

Respectfully submitted,

Stephen T. Elder

Stephen T. Elder
Suite 412
First Savings Building
London, West York 77002
666-1111
Attorney for Plaintiff

ANSWER ON THE MERITS

IN THE UNITED STATES DISTRICT COURT
FOR THE MIDDLE DISTRICT OF WEST YORK
LONDON DIVISION

MIRANDA DOMINGUEZ, Plaintiff	)	
v.	)	NO. CA-71-4683
SCOTT'S FOOD STORES, INC., Defendant	)	

DEFENDANT'S ANSWER

Comes now Scott's Food Stores, Inc., and for an answer to Plaintiff's Complaint would respectfully show the court as follows:

34

FIRST DEFENSE

1. Defendant admits the allegations of paragraph one of the complaint.

2. Defendant admits the allegations of paragraph two of the complaint.

3. Defendant denies that Plaintiff is legally entitled to any damages, but admits that an accident occurred at the date and location alleged in paragraph 3 of the complaint.

4. Defendant admits the allegations of paragraph 4.

5. Defendant denies the allegations of paragraph 5.

6. Defendant is without knowledge or information sufficient to form a belief as to the truth of the allegations of paragraph 6 and therefore must deny same.

7. Defendant is without knowledge or information sufficient to form a belief as to the truth of the allegations of paragraph 7 and therefore must deny same.

8. Defendant admits the allegations of paragraph 8.

9. Defendant denies the allegations of paragraph 9.

10. Defendant admits that Plaintiff has incurred certain charges for medical services and has incurred physical pain as a result of the occurrence in question. Defendant is without sufficient knowledge or information to form a belief as to the truth of the remaining allegations of the first sentence of paragraph 10 and therefore must deny same. Defendant denies the allegations of the second sentence of paragraph 10.

SECOND DEFENSE

11. For further and special answer herein, if such be necessary, and in the alternative, this Defendant avers that such injuries and damages as Plaintiff may have sustained were proximately caused by the failure of Plaintiff to exercise that degree of care which would have been exercised by persons of ordinary prudence in the exercise of ordinary care under the same or similar circumstances.

CONCLUSION AND PRAYER

Wherefore, Defendant prays that Plaintiff take nothing of Defendant, and that Defendant recover its costs.

JURY DEMAND

Defendant respectfully demands trial by jury of all issues so triable.

Respectfully submitted,

McIntosh & Walker

by Robert L. Livingston, Jr.
First City National Bank Bldg.
London, West York 77002

H. NOTES AND QUESTIONS ON FINAL PLEADINGS

1. TIMING OF AMENDED PLEADINGS. Plaintiff was able to obtain an extension of time for filing the amended complaint until after the deposition was taken. Why was this extension helpful?

2. TACTICAL USE OF SPECIFICITY AS VS. BREADTH IN THE AMENDED PLEADING. Although it is permissible to plead generally under the federal standard of "notice" pleading, it may be advantageous to plead more specifically. The reason: a defendant is required to admit or deny each allegation and must do so in good faith. Thus it often makes sense to allege a given fact quite specifically in the complaint, and to set it forth distinctly in a separately numbered paragraph. Note that the answer, in typical fashion, follows the paragraph numbers of the plaintiff's complaint, with admissions or denials addressed to each.

However, with the general outlines of the claim or claims themselves, it may still remain a good tactic to plead generally and inclusively. The reason: the proof often develops unpredictably at trial, and an unduly confining allegation of a claim may create a variance between allegation and proof. (Although the federal rules are relatively liberal in allowing the possibility of amendment even during or after trial, see Fed. R. Civ. P. 18, it is best from a tactical standpoint not to be required to seek permission from the judge at that point.) The pleading of a case so as to use specificity when it is tactically best, and breadth when it is tactically best, is a skill attorneys learn from experience.

3. DEFENDANT'S ANSWER. The answer filed in response to the amended pleading follows the form of Federal Rule 8, with an admission or denial of each allegation. Notice that there are two kinds of defenses: first, admissions and denials, and second, a plea of contributory negligence. Why is contributory negligence specifically and separately pled?

4. JURY DEMAND BY DEFENDANT. Instinctively, we tend to think of juries as more pro-plaintiff than judges. Why, then, is it the defendant that has demanded a jury here? (Hint: It may be that our initial bias—the assumption that juries favor plaintiffs—is erroneous. Additionally, defendant's attorney has years of experience, and plaintiff's attorney is newly licensed; which type of fact finder, judge or jury, would be more affected by experience and skill? Finally, plaintiff's liability evidence is so thin that a challenge to its legal sufficiency may succeed, and it is in defendant's interest to enforce rules excluding evidence as rigorously as possible. Defendant's attorney may suspect that, as a practical matter, it is easier to enforce exclusionary rules of evidence in a trial before a jury than before a judge alone.)

ADDENDUM TO CHAPTER THREE:
IS THE CASE APPROPRIATE FOR SUMMARY JUDGMENT?

I. MOTION FOR SUMMARY JUDGMENT*

---

* No motion for summary judgment was filed in the real case from which this book was taken, and these materials were simulated with the assistance of the attorneys.

DEFENDANT'S MOTION FOR SUMMARY JUDGMENT

IN THE UNITED STATES DISTRICT COURT
FOR THE MIDDLE DISTRICT OF WEST YORK
LONDON DIVISION

MIRANDA DOMINGUEZ, Plaintiff   )
v.   ) NO. CA-71-4683
SCOTT'S FOOD STORES, INC., Defendant)

DEFENDANT'S MOTION FOR SUMMARY JUDGMENT

  Comes now Scott's Food Stores Inc., Defendant in the above styled and numbered cause, and moves the Court, in accordance with Rule 56, for summary judgment, and in support thereof states:
  1. That the pleadings, depositions, answers to interrogatories, and admissions on file, together with the affidavits, if any, show that there is no genuine issue as to any material fact and that Defendant is therefore entitled to judgment as a matter of law.
  2. That in further support thereof, Defendant refers the Court to the accompanying brief.
  Wherefore, Defendant prays that summary judgment be entered that Plaintiff take nothing and that Defendant recover its costs.

           Respectfully submitted,

           Robert L. Livingston, Jr.
           McIntosh & Walker
           by Robert L. Livingston, Jr.
           First City National Bank Bldg.
           London, West York 77002

DEFENDANT'S BRIEF IN SUPPORT OF MOTION FOR SUMMARY JUDGMENT

IN THE UNITED STATES DISTRICT COURT
FOR THE MIDDLE DISTRICT OF WEST YORK
LONDON DIVISION

MIRANDA DOMINGUEZ, Plaintiff   )
v.   ) NO. CA-71-4683
SCOTT'S FOOD STORES, INC., Defendant)

DEFENDANT'S BRIEF IN SUPPORT OF MOTION FOR SUMMARY JUDGMENT

  Defendant recognizes that, pursuant to Rule 56, it has the burden of demonstrating that there are no genuine issues of material fact that could result in judgment for plaintiff and that defendant is entitled to judgment as a matter of law.
  Plaintiff's pleading claims that defendant was negligent in one single respect: that defendant allegedly "crammed [its] bent and broken carts together [and] failed to make sure that they were in sufficiently good repair so that an elderly lady could pull a single cart away from a row." The summary judgment materials, which consist principally of the deposition of the plaintiff, demonstrate

that there is no reasonable way that plaintiff could prevail on these allegations at a trial.

I. THE APPLICABLE LEGAL STANDARD

The applicable substantive law in this diversity case is the law of the State of West York, pursuant to the principles of Erie RR. Co. v. Tompkins, 304 U.S. 64 (1938).

The law of West York is to the effect that, at trial, plaintiff must prove an act of negligence by legally sufficient evidence. With respect to a dangerous condition, there must be sufficient evidence of an act or omission by the defendant such that it either created the dangerous condition, or negligently allowed it to be created, or failed to correct it after an unreasonably long period of time. See Corbin v. Safeway Stores Inc., 648 S.W.2d 297 (W.Y. 1973) (plaintiff cannot recover merely by attributing fall to grape on floor, but must show negligence with respect to grape's presence). If defendant can demonstrate the absence of a reasonable possibility of plaintiff's making such proof, it is entitled to summary judgment.

II. THE FACTS SHOWN BY THE SUMMARY JUDGMENT MATERIALS

In her deposition, plaintiff testified that she pulled on one of the carts in Defendant's store and that three or four baskets came out "and they pushed me down." Deposition of Miranda Dominguez at 27 (hereinafter "Dominguez"). Upon being asked whether she knew why the baskets stuck together, she answered, "No." Id. Upon being asked whether she had any idea why they allegedly stuck, she again said, "No, sir." When asked whether she ever made any inspection of the baskets, she testified, "No, sir." Dominguez 28. Finally, she was asked whether she knew why the baskets had stuck together, and she answered, "No, sir." Dominguez 30.

There were no other witnesses, and this evidence is the only evidence that is available about the alleged reason for the alleged "sticking" of the baskets. Plaintiff testified that "there was nobody there," and when asked whether there was anybody "in the immediate area who saw the fall," she testified, "No, sir, I don't think so. I didn't see anybody there, sir." Dominguez 30.

CONCLUSION

Defendant has demonstrated the absence of a reasonable possibility that plaintiff could prevail at trial, even if plaintiff is given the benefit of the most favorable inferences from the evidence. There is thus no genuine issue of material fact, and defendant is entitled to judgment as a matter of law.

Respectfully submitted,

Robert L. Livingston, Jr.

McIntosh & Walker

by Robert L. Livinston, Jr.
First City National Bank Bldg.
London, West York 77002

IN THE UNITED STATES DISTRICT COURT
FOR THE MIDDLE DISTRICT OF WEST YORK
LONDON DIVISION

MIRANDA DOMINGUEZ, Plaintiff)
v.)   NO. CA-71-4683
SCOTT'S FOOD STORES, INC., Defendant)

PLAINTIFF'S BRIEF IN OPPOSITION TO SUMMARY JUDGMENT

Summary judgment can be granted only if there are no genuine issues of material fact. Although plaintiff might have the burden of proof at trial, the Movant--Scott's Foods--bears a heavy burden, in this summary judgment proceeding, of demonstrating that there is no reasonable way plaintiff can make that proof at a trial. Fed. R. Civ. P. 56; see generally Adickes v. S. H. Kress & Co., 398 U.S. 144, 159-60 (1970) (it is the "burden of the moving party" to show "the absence of a genuine issue concerning any material facts").

I.   THE APPLICABLE LEGAL PRINCIPLES

The applicable substantive law does not require, as defendant's brief implies, that negligence must be proved solely and directly by an eyewitness. Here there does happen to be such direct testimony, and some of it is cited below; but West York also recognizes that negligence may be proved circumstantially. For example, West York recognizes the principle of "res ipsa loquitur," meaning "the thing speaks for itself," whereby an inference of negligence may be drawn even if there is no direct evidence of an act of negligence at all. See Mobil Chemical Co. v. Bell, 517 S.W.2d 245 (W.Y. 1974). The requisite elements for application of res ipsa loquitur are (1) that the instrumentality from which the accident results must be in the control of the defendant (and here, defendant controlled its carts) and (2) that the accident must be of a type that ordinarily would not occur without negligence (and here, the carts stuck so that three or four came out together). Id.

II.   THE FACTS SHOWN BY SUMMARY JUDGMENT MATERIALS

The record simply does not demonstrate that plaintiff will be unable to show negligence. For instance, plaintiff's deposition contains her detailed testimony that the carts were crammed together "too tight." Dominguez 27. The evidence further showed that, in general, defendant allowed its carts to be left in the rain, played with by children who ran them into each other, and abandoned throughout the neighborhood. The record shows that the carts were bent, were old and rundown, and were not repaired or replaced regularly. Dominguez 30-31. All of this evidence demonstrates Defendant's negligence.

CONCLUSION

Defendant has failed to carry its heavy burden of demonstrating the absence of a reasonable possibility of plaintiff's prevailing at trial. The motion for summary judgment should be denied.

Respectfully submitted,

Stephen T. Elder
_____
Stephen T. Elder
711 Fannin Street
London, West York 77002

NOTE ON COURT'S ORDER DENYING SUMMARY JUDGMENT

The court denied the motion without a hearing. Remember that in many cases this court followed the practice of ruling on motions after a submission date without oral argument. In fact, many courts follow this practice in summary judgment cases in which a hearing would not be helpful; see Rule 78.

J. NOTES AND QUESTIONS ON MOTION FOR SUMMARY JUDGMENT

1. **SHOULD THE MOTION HAVE BEEN FILED?** In the real case from which this book is taken, no motion for summary judgment was actually filed; these particular materials were simulated by the authors with the aid of the attorneys. Why do you think the real defendant did not file such a motion?

2. **RULE 11: THE "REASONABLENESS-IN-PLEADINGS-AND-MOTIONS" RULE.** Fed. R. Civ. P. 11 requires an attorney to do a "reasonable investigation" of both the facts and the law to ensure that the facts have evidentiary support and that nonfrivolous argument justifies the filing. The court can impose sanctions upon a person responsible for violating the Rule (at least one who persists in the violation). Could such a rule deter motions like this Motion for Summary Judgment? If it did, would the streamlining of the process and the lowered cost be desirable?

3. **STANDARDS FOR SUMMARY JUDGMENT.** At trial, plaintiff will have the burden of proving negligence. But the standard for granting or denying summary judgment is different from the standard for prevailing at trial, as the briefs recognize. What is the standard, and is it properly applied here?

4. **THE PARTIES' USE OF LEGAL REASONING: FIRST, RECOGNITION OF THE ISSUES; SECOND, LEGAL PRINCIPLES; THIRD, ANALYSIS OF FACTS; FOURTH, CONCLUSION.** Notice how the briefs are structured. After identifying the issue, each sets out the applicable legal principles, including relevant refinements, qualifications or limits on those principles. Each brief then enumerates and analyzes the facts shown by the record, comparing them to the legal standard. Finally, these elements are used to draw a conclusion. At least in cases in which the law is reasonably clear (as here), this approach is characteristic of good legal reasoning.

It may interest you to know that a similar approach is often advocated as a means of answering law school examinations. The student first identifies the issue, then gives the "rule" (or applicable legal principles), then does an analysis of the facts, and finally draws a conclusion. This issue-rule-analysis-conclusion sequence is sometimes referred to as the "IRAC" method. You may find it satisfying to see that it has real application in legal arguments!

5. **THE APPLICABLE SUBSTANTIVE LAW; THE "ERIE" DOCTRINE.** As the briefs indicate, the court is required to follow state substantive law in deciding a suit in which jurisdiction is founded on diversity of citizenship. The court follows federal procedural law. These principles were established in the landmark case of *Erie RR. Co. v. Tompkins*, 304 U.S. 64 (1938).

CHAPTER FOUR:

LATER PRETRIAL PROCEEDINGS

A. JOINT PRETRIAL ORDER PROPOSAL

THE DRAFT PRETRIAL ORDER
IN THE UNITED STATES DISTRICT COURT
FOR THE MIDDLE DISTRICT OF WEST YORK
LONDON DIVISION

```
MIRANDA DOMINGUEZ, Plaintiff       )
v.                                 )        NO. CA-71-4683
SCOTT'S FOOD STORES, INC., Defendant )
```

STANDARD JOINT PRETRIAL ORDER

APPEARANCE OF COUNSEL

Stephen T. Elder, Suite 412, First Savings Building, London, West York 77002, 666-1111, is the attorney for plaintiff Miranda Dominguez. Robert L. Livingston, Jr., McIntosh & Walker, First City National Bank Building, London, West York 77002, is attorney for defendant Scott's Food Stores, Inc.

STATEMENT OF THE CASE

Plaintiff sustained a broken wrist at Scott's Food Store No. 14 on Quitman Street in London, Manero County, West York, on May 7, 1996, and she here sues for damages which she claims are due to the alleged negligence of defendant.

JURISDICTION

The court has jurisdiction pursuant to 28 U.S.C. 1332 (diversity of citizenship).

MOTIONS

Defendant has filed a Motion in Limine, a copy of which is attached hereto. There are no other pending motions.

CONTENTIONS OF THE PARTIES

Plaintiff contends that defendant negligently maintained its premises in that its carts were defective, were crammed together too tightly, and were negligently repaired, and that such negligence was the proximate cause of damage in the form of past and future medical expenses, pain and suffering, and lost ability to conduct housekeeping services, as well as other damage. Plaintiff contends she was not guilty of any contributory negligence. Defendant contends that it was not negligent, that no negligence on its part was a proximate cause of any damage, and that plaintiff was contributorily negligent in failing to exercise reasonable care for her own safety in her use or attempted use of defendant's grocery carts.

ADMISSIONS OF FACT AND CONTESTED ISSUES OF FACT

A. It is stipulated between the parties that an incident did occur on May 7, 1996, involving plaintiff, in the Scott's Food Store No. 14, and that plaintiff did suffer injury therefrom. It is further stipulated that defendant, through its employees, owned and maintained grocery carts in question, and that it furnished the carts for the use of patrons, including Miranda Dominguez.

B. The contested issues of fact include defendant's alleged negligence, proximate causation from defendant's negligence, plaintiff's negligence, proximate causation from plaintiff's negligence, and the extent of damage proximately caused, if any.

AGREED APPLICABLE PROPOSITIONS OF LAW
AND CONTESTED ISSUES OF LAW

A. The parties agree that West York law defining negligence, proximate causation, ordinary care, and amount of damage, is applicable to the case.

B. No contested issues of law are known to the parties at this time.

EXHIBITS

Exhibits proposed by plaintiff include (1) medical records of Dr. Ralph Ellman and (2) medical records of County Memorial Hospital, both pertaining to plaintiff. Defendant objects and excepts to the admissibility and authenticity of such exhibits in that they contain multiple level hearsay not constituting business records or other hearsay exceptions, and that they contain material whose source and method of preparation indicate lack of trustworthiness not satisfying the reliability requirements of the federal rules of evidence. Defendant proposes to offer, as an exhibit, (1) records of repair of baskets by Scott's Food Sotres, Inc. in London, West York, and (2) records of purchase of such bascarts. This designation does not include rebuttal exhibits which cannot be anticipated.

WITNESSES

Plaintiff proposes to offer as witnesses Miranda Dominguez, 2944 Dunham (to testify concerning the circumstances of injury and damages); Edward Dominguez, same address, Thelma Rodriguez, 1801 Shepard; and Mrs. Joe E. Martinez, 2018 Timber (to testify concerning the condition of defendant's premises, and the nature of plaintiff's injuries and damages).

Defendant expects to call Wayne Douglas, c/o Scott's Food Stores, Inc., and George Franklin, same address (to testify concerning defendant's maintenance of its premises and baskets).

As required by Local Rules, the following statement is added: "In the event there are other witnesses to be called at the trial, their names, addresses and the subject matter of their testimony shall be reported to opposing counsel as soon as they are known. This restriction shall not apply to rebuttal or impeaching witnesses, the necessity of whose testimony cannot reasonably be anticipated before the time of trial."

SETTLEMENT

In accordance with Local Rules, the parties include the following statement: "All settlement efforts have been exhausted, the case cannot be settled, and it will have to be tried."

TRIAL

The probable length of trial is one to two days. There are no out of state witnesses, and it is expected that all witnesses will be available, with the possible exception of subpoenaed witnesses.

Owing to the nature of the case, the parties have requested that the requirement of a fully drafted proposed charge to the jury from each side, including instructions or definitions and proposed special interrogatories, be waived. Owing to the nature of the case, the parties have requested the court that the requirement of submission of proposed questions for voir dire examination of the jury panel be waived, and that the parties be enabled to conduct the examination.

John T. Hughes
United States District Judge

Approval recommended:

Stephen T. Elder
Attorney for Plaintiff

Robert L. Livingston Jr.
Attorney for Defendant

B. THE PROCESS OF SCHEDULING THE CASE FOR TRIAL

NOTE ON SETTING
THE CASE FOR TRIAL

Different jurisdictions often use different systems for setting trials. Unless the jurisdiction is close and familiar, many attorneys follow the practice of engaging local counsel. Again, this process shows the importance of local rules and of scheduling.

The process used by the Middle District of West York is unusual among federal courts. The attorneys initiate trial settings by filing trial setting requests on forms provided by the court. Each week, the docket clerk of the district prepares a list of all cases in which setting requests have been received. The order is by age of the case, or in order of increasing docket numbers. Thus the oldest case is given number 1, the next oldest 2, and so forth. The district judges, beginning with case number 1, are assigned the cases for trial. The weekly list often includes many more cases than can reasonably be expected to be tried, but since trial settings precipitate settlement or continuance in most cases, the courts are able to dispose of many more than might be expected. Those cases for which setting requests are filed but which are not reached require further setting requests in the future.

This process is subject to criticism. The judge who ruled on pleading and discovery questions will probably not be the same judge who presides over the trial, so that precious resources are wasted as the "new" judge learns about the case. Judges also have less incentive to make definitive pretrial rulings (since the effect on their own individual dockets is insignificant). Further, the process often leads to multiple resettings of a given case, discouraging careful preparation and creating difficulties for parties and witnesses. A more typical federal procedure is the initiation of trial settings by the judge, together with vigorous use of pretrial conferences.

FIRST TRIAL SETTING REQUEST FORM

UNITED STATES DISTRICT COURT FOR THE
MIDDLE DISTRICT OF WEST YORK, LONDON DIVISION

MIRANDA DOMINGUEZ

V.

SCOTT'S FOOD STORES, INC.

JURY / NON-JURY

NO. _CA-71-4683_

TO THE DISTRICT CLERK: Please set the above titled and numbered cause for trial on the General Docket for Monday, September 20, 1998, or such time during the week thereafter as may be possible for the court.

In accordance with Rule 3 of the Local Rules of this Court, I, the undersigned, hereby certify as follows: (a) that the pleadings are in order; (b) that counsel upon whom this request for setting is served has not withdrawn from the case; (c) that all necessary matters preliminary to trial have been accomplished; (d) that a proposed pretrial order conforming to the requirements of Local Rule 12 has been filed; and (e) THAT I HAVE IN GOOD FAITH NEGOTIATED TO SETTLE THE CASE AND HAVE COMMUNICATED MY BEST OFFER TO EACH OTHER PARTY IN WRITING.

Names and addresses of all counsel   _Robert L. Livingston Jr._
appear on the reverse hereof   signature of party so certifying

NOTE ON MULTIPLE RESETTING OF
CASE FOR TRIAL

During the pendency of the suit, Mr. Livingston notified his client that certain persons, including the store manager and a customer who could testify that the grocery carts were new at the time of the accident, would be helpful witnesses at trial. The case was not tried during the week requested in the first setting form above. In fact, multiple setting requests were filed and the case was not tried until September 2000. By that time, both the manager and the assistant manager of the store had left the defendant's employ, and no customer could be found who recalled the condition of the carts at the time of the accident.

The following trial setting requests were filed by defense counsel. Following each filing, an excerpt of a letter from defense counsel to his client appears, advising of the new setting and trial docket number.

UNITED STATES DISTRICT COURT FOR THE
MIDDLE DISTRICT OF WEST YORK, LONDON DIVISION

MIRANDA DOMINGUEZ

V.   JURY / NON-JURY

SCOTT'S FOOD STORES, INC.   NO. CA-71-4683

TO THE DISTRICT CLERK: Please set the above titled and numbered cause for trial on the General Docket for Monday, February 5, 2000.
* * *

Upon being notified of the sequence number assigned the case, defense counsel wrote his client:

> * * *
> This case appears as No. 225 on the jury docket for the week of February 5, 2000. There is not much chance of the case going to trial but at the time of trial we will need the store manager of Store No. 14 and the custodian of the bascart purchase records for Scott's Food Stores. * * *

The case was not reached for trial by the court on the February 5 setting. Mr. Livingston filed the following:

UNITED STATES DISTRICT COURT FOR THE
MIDDLE DISTRICT OF WEST YORK, LONDON DIVISION

MIRANDA DOMINGUEZ

V.

SCOTT'S FOOD STORES, INC.

JURY / NON-JURY

NO. CA-71-4683

TO THE DISTRICT CLERK: Please set the above titled and numbered cause for trial on the General Docket for Monday, March 12, 2000.
* * *

Defense counsel wrote:

* * *

This case is set for trial during the week of March 12, 2000, and appears as No. 186 on the jury docket for that week. There is a slight chance the case will be reached for trial at that setting. * * *

Again, when the case was not reached for trial, Mr. Livingston filed the following and wrote the following letter:

UNITED STATES DISTRICT COURT FOR THE
MIDDLE DISTRICT OF WEST YORK, LONDON DIVISION

MIRANDA DOMINGUEZ

V.

SCOTT'S FOOD STORES, INC.

JURY / NON-JURY

NO. CA-71-4683

TO THE DISTRICT CLERK: Please set the above titled and numbered cause for trial on the General Docket for Monday, July 16, 2000.
* * *

* * *

This case is set for trial during the week of July 16, 2000, and appears as No. 96 on the docket for that week. This case will in all probability be reached for trial at that time. * * *

Again, however, the case was not tried; Mr. Livingston wrote:

* * *

The captioned cause did not get assigned a number on the week of July 16, 2000, because Mr. Elder, the attorney for the plaintiff, had a vacation letter on file. We will set this case for trial during the September-October term of court.
* * *

Pursuant to his letter, Mr. Livingston filed the following:

UNITED STATES DISTRICT COURT FOR THE
MIDDLE DISTRICT OF WEST YORK, LONDON DIVISION

MIRANDA DOMINGUEZ
V.

SCOTT'S FOOD STORES, INC.

JURY / NON-JURY

NO. CA-71-4683

TO THE DISTRICT CLERK: Please set the above titled and numbered cause for trial on the General Docket for Monday, September 17, 2000.
* * *

The case was finally tried in September of 2000. (To the student who is understandably surprised by the apparent waste of effort inherent in such resettings, it should be pointed out that the setting requests are changed only as to parties' names and format; these were the actual dates requested and the actual trial assignments in the case.) Some method must be used to assign cases to trial. This trial-and-error method seems cumbersome, but it is better than it might appear: the attorneys know their schedules and they can initiate settings by a simple form. There are methods that many consider more efficient (such as the assignment of pretrial and trial to a single judge), but this "request" method is not unique, and the experience of these litigants in having trials repeatedly rescheduled is not unusual, whatever system a given court uses.

C. PROCEEDINGS ON THE EVE OF TRIAL

MOTION IN LIMINE

IN THE UNITED STATES DISTRICT COURT
FOR THE MIDDLE DISTRICT OF WEST YORK
LONDON DIVISION

MIRANDA DOMINGUEZ, Plaintiff)
v.) NO. CA-71-4683
SCOTT'S FOOD STORES, INC., Defendant)

DEFENDANT'S MOTION IN LIMINE

Comes now Scott's Food Stores, Inc., Defendant, and before the trial of the above entitled and numbered cause, before voir dire examination of the jury, and before receipt of any evidence makes this, its Motion in Limine, and would respectfully show unto the Court:

I.

Defendant moves the Court to instruct counsel for Plaintiff to refrain from mentioning, either directly or indirectly, in response to Defendant's suggestion or otherwise, any of the matters set forth in the proposed form of order herein, unless a prior ruling be obtained from the court, for the reason that such matters are excluded by provisions of the Federal Rules of Evidence, and contemporaneous objection to a question or other remark will not prevent the inference of such matters by the jury.

WHEREFORE, premises considered, Defendant moves the Court to enter the attached form of order and to instruct counsel for Plaintiff in accordance therewith.

Respectfully submitted,

MCINTOSH & WALKER

By _Robert L. Livingston Jr._
Robert L. Livingston, Jr.
First City National Bank Bldg.
London, West York   77002

ATTORNEYS FOR DEFENDANT

ORDER ON MOTION IN LIMINE

BE IT REMEMBERED on this day came on to be heard Defendant's Motion in Limine and the Court, after considering such Motion, is of the opinion that it should be and it is hereby sustained, and Counsel for Plaintiff is hereby ordered to refrain from mentioning, either directly or indirectly, any of the following matters in the presence or hearing of the jurors, except as herein provided:

1. That liability insurance will or will not indemnify defendant for any part of any damage recovered against it, if any; and

2. That defendant or plaintiff has or has not made or passed upon any offer of compromise, settlement, or payment in this case or any other case;

and in the event Plaintiff's counsel should consider that any such remarks are proper in the context of the evidence as it develops, he shall first approach the bench and obtain a ruling from the court out of the presence and out of the hearing of the jurors.

SIGNED, RENDERED and ENTERED this _1st_ day of _Sept._, _2000_ .

John T. Hughes
JUDGE PRESIDING

SUBPOENA TO MEDICAL RECORDS CUSTODIAN

United States District Court

FOR THE

MIDDLE DISTRICT OF WEST YORK, LONDON DIVISION

MIRANDA DOMINGUEZ

vs.

SCOTT'S FOOD STORES, INC.

CIVIL ACTION FILE No.   CA-71-4683

To Ralph Ellman, custodian of
    the records of Ralph Ellman,
    or his designated custodian

YOU ARE HEREBY COMMANDED to appear in the United States District Court for the Middle District of West York, London Division , at 515 Rusk Street in the city of London, West York on the 17th day of September 2000 at 8:45 o'clock A. M. to testify on behalf of plaintiff in the above entitled action and bring with you

medical records of Miranda Dominguez.

This subpoena shall remain in effect until you are granted leave to depart by the court or by an officer acting on behalf of the court.

Sept. 13, _____ , 2000 .
Stephen T. Elder
_____
Attorney for Plaintiff
First Savings Bldg., London
_____
Address

W.B. Lewis
_____ ,
Clerk.
By *Brenda Morgan*
Brenda Morgan Deputy Clerk.

RETURN ON SERVICE

Received this subpoena at   3:00 P.M.   on   September 13, 2000,
and on   Sept. 14, 2000 at   9:30 A.M.,
Served it on the within named   Ralph Ellman
by delivering a copy to him and tendering to him the fee for one day's attendance and the mileage allowed by law.[1]

Dated:
Sept. 14, _____ , 2000
Service Fees
    Travel_____ $ 1.00
    Services_____ 1.00

    Total _____ $ 2.00

Candace Welch
_____ ,
By _____

Subscribed and sworn to before me, at   London, W.Y.,   this   14th
day of   September   , 2000.
W. B. Bockius,
Notary Public in and for West York

[1] Fees and mileage need not be tendered to the witness upon service of a subpoena issued in behalf of the United States or an officer or agency thereof.   28 USC 1825.

NOTE. — Affidavit required only if service is made by a person other than a United States Marshal or his deputy.

NOTE ON PRETRIAL CONFERENCE
REFERENCES TO THE FEDERAL
RULES OF EVIDENCE

In the excerpts from the pretrial conference that follow, there are several references to the Federal Rules of Evidence, particularly Rule 803(6).

Rule 803(6) is a part of the treatment of hearsay in the Rules of Evidence. Hearsay evidence is excluded by the rules. This exclusion applies not only to spoken hearsay but also to written documents that embody hearsay. However, there are exceptions to the hearsay rule. Rule 803(6) embodies one of these exceptions, applicable to records of "regularly conducted" activity. The Rule is intended to allow introduction into evidence of such business records as accounting books, medical records, and the like.

EXCERPT FROM TRANSCRIPT OF FINAL PRETRIAL HEARING

IN CHAMBERS

* * *

MR. LIVINGSTON: The Defendant, Scott's Food Store, stipulates that the medical records meet the requirements of Federal Rule of Evidence 803(6), except insofar as such records contain indications on their face showing noncompliance with the requirements of 803(6). Defendant expressly does not stipulate to the admissibility of any except to the extent indicated.

[Exhibits Nos. 1 (the narrative summary from Dr. Ellman to Plaintiff's lawyer), 2 (treatment records of Plaintiff by Dr. Ellman), 3 (Memorial Hospital records of Plaintiff), and 4 (correspondence by Dr. Ellman to plaintiff), were marked for identification by the reporter.]

MR. ELDER: Your Honor, we offer into evidence what have been marked Plaintiff's Exhibits 1 through 4.

MR. LIVINGSTON: Defendant objects to Plaintiff's Exhibit No. 1 in toto. The exhibit purports to be a letter addressed to plaintiff's lawyer from plaintiff's doctor, Ralph Ellman, setting out Ms. Dominguez's treatment by Dr. Ellman taken from his medical records, and it constitutes hearsay as to this Defendant. It is not a part of the business records of the physician, but is prepared in anticipation of litigation, and as such, it is not admissible under the business records provision, Rule 803(6). The medical records themselves might be admissible for whatever purpose they might serve, but a letter prepared from those documents to a party for the very purpose of advancing a lawsuit is just out-and-out hearsay.

THE COURT: Sustained.

MR. ELDER: We offer Plaintiff's 1 in the form of an offer of proof. * * *

[At this point, there are approximately 18 pages of transcript containing arguments and rulings on evidence. For example, Mr. Livingston successfully objects on relevancy grounds to a number of references to prior injuries or illnesses of Mrs. Dominguez. He unsuccessfully objects on relevancy grounds to an x-ray report that he claims is intelligible only to physicians.]

MR. LIVINGSTON: Defendant, Scott's Food Store, objects to Plaintiff's Exhibit No. 4 and, more specifically, that portion which states "Insurance, Connecticut General Thru Williams" in that such is simply an attempt to inject into the evidence of this case that some partial insurance recovery may or may not have been obtained by the Plaintiff and that Plaintiff still owes a substantial medical bill over and above insurance; such matter as contained on the first page of Plaintiff's Exhibit No. 4 being wholly irrelevant and immaterial to any issue to be submitted to the jury.

THE COURT: The objection is sustained. * * *

[The Court granted permission to Mr. Livingston to offer his exhibits during trial, on the representation that they were intended to rebut Plaintiff's evidence, and would be used only if they were determined necessary.]

THE COURT: On the motion in limine: it seems to me that defendant is right and I'm going to grant it.

In addition, I'm going to enter the joint proposed pretrial order that you filed earlier in this case, subject to and including the evidence rulings made here in this conference. All evidence offered is hereby admitted, except for those documents or parts of documents to which objections were sustained. * * *

CHAPTER FIVE:

THE TRIAL

A. JURY SELECTION

JUROR INFORMATION FORMS OF THE PANEL

JUROR NO. 275-17   JUROR INFORMATION FORM   PLEASE TYPE OR PRINT IN BLACK INK

Single/Husband or Wife's Name	How long have you lived in County 20	No. of Children 2	Phone No. 222-1212	Zip Code 77733	Your Age 51
Mary Gunther	Your present Employer Continental Can Company	No. of years worked there 20		What is your type of work? operator	
Your place of birth Washington County, West York	Your Husband or Wife's Employer Gulfgate State Bank	No. of years worked there 14		What is their type of work? Proof Supervisor	

Have you ever served on a Civil Jury? **X** Yes ☐ No   Have you ever served on a Criminal Jury? ☐ Yes **X** No

Have you ever been party to a Law Suit? ☐ Yes **X** No   If yes, what type?

Any accidental bodily injury ever sustained requiring medical attention?
By you? ☐ Yes **X** No   By your family? ☐ Yes **X** No
If so, type of injury by you   If so, type of injury by your family

Signature: *Lyle K. Gunther*

JUROR NO. 275-17
GUNTHER, LYLE K. ③

JUROR NO. 281-17   JUROR INFORMATION FORM   PLEASE TYPE OR PRINT IN BLACK INK

Single/Husband or Wife's Name	How long have you lived in County 54y	No. of Children 3	Phone No. 471-6000	Zip Code 77571	Your Age 54
Single	Your present Employer LaPorte Ind. School. Dist 7			What is your type of work? Cafteria Manger	
Your place of birth Morgan's Point, Fla.	Your Husband or Wife's Employer	No. of years worked there		What is their type of work?	

Have you ever served on a Civil Jury? ☐ Yes **X** No   Have you ever served on a Criminal Jury? ☐ Yes **X** No

Have you ever been party to a Law Suit? ☐ Yes **X** No   If yes, what type?

Any accidental bodily injury ever sustained requiring medical attention?
By you? ☐ Yes **X** No   By your family? ☐ Yes **X** No
If so, type of injury by you   If so, type of injury by your family

Signature: *Clara Jane Walston*

JUROR NO. 281-17
WALSTON, CLARA JANE ④

JUROR INFORMATION FORM   PLEASE TYPE OR PRINT IN BLACK INK

Single/Husband or Wife's Name	How long have you lived in County 30 yrs	No. of Children 1	Phone No. 993-1635	Zip Code 77029	Your Age 56
RALPH SCOTT	Your present Employer RETIRED City of LONDON 30 yrs			What is your type of work? Public HEALTH NURSE	
Your place of birth LAVALLA WEST YORK	Your Husband or Wife's Employer RETIRED FEDERAL RESERVE BANK 20 yrs			What is their type of work? Guard	

Have you ever served on a Civil Jury? **X** Yes ☐ No   Have you ever served on a Criminal Jury? ☐ Yes **X** No

Have you ever been party to a Law Suit? ☐ Yes **X** No   If yes, what type?

Any accidental bodily injury ever sustained requiring medical attention?
By you? ☐ Yes **X** No   By your family? ☐ Yes **X** No
If so, type of injury by you   If so, type of injury by your family

Signature: *Mrs. Vera Scott*

JUROR NO. 284-17
SCOTT, VERA ⑤

JUROR NO. 288-17   JUROR INFORMATION FORM   PLEASE TYPE OR PRINT IN BLACK INK

Single/Husband or Wife's Name	How long have you lived in County 30 yr	No. of Children 4	Phone No. 692-5555	Zip Code 77022	Your Age 43
Linda Goedecke	Your present Employer Automatic Power, Inc	6 mo		What is your type of work? Accounting	
Your place of birth Fayetteville Ark.	Your Husband or Wife's Employer NO	None		What is their type of work?	

Have you ever served on a Civil Jury? ☐ Yes **X** No   Have you ever served on a Criminal Jury? ☐ Yes **X** No

Have you ever been party to a Law Suit? ☐ Yes **X** No   If yes, what type?

Any accidental bodily injury ever sustained requiring medical attention?
By you? ☐ Yes **X** No   By your family? ☐ Yes **X** No
If so, type of injury by you   If so, type of injury by your family

Signature: *J. M. Goedecke III*

JUROR NO. 288-17
GOEDECKE, J.M. III ⑥

53

Single/Husband or Wife's Name	How long have you lived in County	No. of Children	Phone No.	Zip Code	Your Age
MARK TILLMAN	39	2	222-0240	77008	58

Your present Employer	No. of years worked there ▼	What is your type of work?
NONE		HOUSEWIFE

Your place of birth: TYLER, WEST YORK

Your Husband or Wife's Employer	No. of years worked there ▼	What is their type of work?
RETIRED		FOUNDRY OWNER

Have you ever served on a Civil Jury? ☐ Yes ☑ No
Have you ever served on a Criminal Jury? ☑ Yes ☐ No

Have you ever been party to a Law Suit? ☐ Yes ☑ No   If yes, what type?

Any accidental bodily injury ever sustained requiring medical attention?
By you? ☐ Yes ☑ No   By your family? ☐ Yes ☑ No
If so, type of injury by you   If so, type of injury by your family

Signature: Jenara Lee Tillman

JUROR NO. 291-17
TILLMAN, JENARA LEE
⑦

Single/Husband or Wife's Name	How long have you lived in County	No. of Children	Phone No.	Zip Code	Your Age
Single	12 yrs	-	555-2233	77027	36

Your present Employer	No. of years worked there ▼	What is your type of work?
Exxon Company, U.S.A.	14	Secretary

Your place of birth: Rodessa, West York

Your Husband or Wife's Employer	No. of years worked there ▼	What is their type of work?
-	-	-

Have you ever served on a Civil Jury? ☑ Yes ☐ No
Have you ever served on a Criminal Jury? ☑ Yes ☐ No

Have you ever been party to a Law Suit? ☐ Yes ☑ No   If yes, what type?

Any accidental bodily injury ever sustained requiring medical attention?
By you? ☑ Yes ☐ No   By your family? ☐ Yes ☑ No
If so, type of injury by you: broken wrist-cut face   If so, type of injury by your family: -

Signature: Mary McIver

JUROR NO. 303-17
MCIVER, MARY
⑧

Single/Husband or Wife's Name	How long have you lived in County	No. of Children	Phone No.	Zip Code	Your Age
Betty Furney GREEN	11 yrs	3	465-0078	77024	43

Your present Employer	No. of years worked there ▼	What is your type of work?
West York Chemicals	15	General Mgr.

Your place of birth: Alberta, Canada

Your Husband or Wife's Employer	No. of years worked there ▼	What is their type of work?
		Housewife

Have you ever served on a Civil Jury? ☑ Yes ☐ No
Have you ever served on a Criminal Jury? ☐ Yes ☑ No

Have you ever been party to a Law Suit? ☐ Yes ☑ No   If yes, what type?

Any accidental bodily injury ever sustained requiring medical attention?
By you? ☑ Yes ☐ No   By your family? ☐ Yes ☑ No
If so, type of injury by you: Leg   If so, type of injury by your family

Signature: Robert W. Green

JUROR NO. 310-17
GREEN, ROBERT WAYNE
⑨

Single/Husband or Wife's Name	How long have you lived in County	No. of Children	Phone No.	Zip Code	Your Age
John A Florence	14 yrs	2	999-3434	70002	

Your present Employer	No. of years worked there ▼	What is your type of work?
Brown & Root		

Your place of birth: Ruston, Louisiana

Your Husband or Wife's Employer	No. of years worked there ▼	What is their type of work?

Have you ever served on a Civil Jury? ☐ Yes ☐ No
Have you ever served on a Criminal Jury? ☐ Yes ☐ No

Have you ever been party to a Law Suit? ☐ Yes ☐ No   If yes, what type?

Any accidental bodily injury ever sustained requiring medical attention?
By you? ☐ Yes ☐ No   By your family? ☐ Yes ☐ No
If so, type of injury by you   If so, type of injury by your family

Signature: John A Florence

JUROR NO. 312-17
FLORENCE, JOHN A.
⑩

JUROR INFORMATION FORM — JUROR NO. 221-17

Single/Husband or Wife's Name	How long have you lived in County	No. of Children	Phone No.	Zip Code	Your Age
Charles	12 yrs	3	555-7585	77777	39

Your place of birth: Middletown, Ohio

Your present Employer: Self Holland Center Beauty Salon 9 yrs / What is your type of work? Beautician

Your Husband or Wife's Employer: Vernon Court Co. / No. of years worked there: 1½ / What is their type of work? Brick Layer

Have you ever served on a Civil Jury? ☐ Yes ☑ No
Have you ever served on a Criminal Jury? ☐ Yes ☑ No

Have you ever been party to a Law Suit? ☐ Yes ☑ No If yes, what type?

Any accidental bodily injury ever sustained requiring medical attention?
By you? ☐ Yes ☑ No By your family? ☐ Yes ☑ No
If so, type of injury by you: If so, type of injury by your family:

Signature: Elaine Delorme

JUROR NO. 221-17
DELORME, ELAINE
⑪

JUROR INFORMATION FORM

Single/Husband or Wife's Name	How long have you lived in County	No. of Children	Phone No.	Zip Code	Your Age
Lloyd	13 yrs	2	444-2222	77017	36

Your place of birth: Bay City

Your present Employer: Center / Hosp. / What is your type of work? Office work

Your Husband or Wife's Employer: / No. of years worked there: / What is their type of work?

Have you ever served on a Civil Jury? ☐ Yes ☐ No
Have you ever served on a Criminal Jury? ☐ Yes ☐ No

Have you ever been party to a Law Suit? ☐ Yes ☐ No If yes, what type?

Any accidental bodily injury ever sustained requiring medical attention?
By you? ☐ Yes ☐ No By your family? ☐ Yes ☐ No
If so, type of injury by you: auto acc - 1 yr   If so, type of injury by your family:

Signature: Jennie C. Tyler

JUROR NO. 223-17
TYLER, JENNIE C.
⑫

JUROR NO. — JUROR INFORMATION FORM

Single/Husband or Wife's Name	How long have you lived in County	No. of Children	Phone No.	Zip Code	Your Age
FRANCES C.	24 YRS	2	333-3146	77017	51

Your place of birth: LUDLOW KENTUCKY

Your present Employer: G & H TOOL & DIE COMPANY / 15 / What is your type of work? PRES.

Your Husband or Wife's Employer: / No. of years worked there: / What is their type of work?

Have you ever served on a Civil Jury? ☑ Yes ☐ No
Have you ever served on a Criminal Jury? ☐ Yes ☑ No

Have you ever been party to a Law Suit? ☐ Yes ☑ No If yes, what type?

Any accidental bodily injury ever sustained requiring medical attention?
By you? ☐ Yes ☑ No By your family? ☐ Yes ☑ No
If so, type of injury by you: If so, type of injury by your family:

Signature: William P. Magnusson

JUROR NO. 2-18
MAGNUSSON, WILLIAM P.
⑬

JUROR NO. — JUROR INFORMATION FORM

Single/Husband or Wife's Name	How long have you lived in County	No. of Children	Phone No.	Zip Code	Your Age
SUSAN CORTELLI	26 YRS	1	686-7777	77018	51

Your place of birth: CHICAGO, WEST YORK

Your present Employer: DANIEL INDUSTRIES, INC. / 0 / What is your type of work? MECH. ENGINEERING

Your Husband or Wife's Employer: HOUSEWIFE / No. of years worked there: / What is their type of work? HOUSEWIFE

Have you ever served on a Civil Jury? ☐ Yes ☑ No
Have you ever served on a Criminal Jury? ☐ Yes ☑ No

Have you ever been party to a Law Suit? ☐ Yes ☑ No If yes, what type?

Any accidental bodily injury ever sustained requiring medical attention?
By you? ☑ Yes ☐ No By your family? ☑ Yes ☐ No
If so, type of injury by you: BROKEN ANKLE   If so, type of injury by your family: CUT LEG

Signature: Philip R. Cortelli

JUROR NO. 313-17
CORTELLI, PHILIP R.
⑭

55

JUROR NO. 316-17   JUROR INFORMATION FORM   [PLEASE TYPE OR PRINT IN BLACK INK]

Single/Husband or Wife's Name	How long have you lived in County 20 YRS.	No. of Children NONE	Phone No. 699-9954	Zip Code 77022	Your Age 20
SARA BROWN	Your present Employer DOYLE'S HARDWARE	No. of years worked there ▼ 3 MO.		What is your type of work? SALESMAN	
Your place of birth	Your Husband or Wife's Employer	No. of years worked there ▼		What is their type of work?	
LONDON, WEST YORK					

Have you ever served on a Civil Jury? ☐ Yes ☒ No   Have you ever served on a Criminal Jury? ☐ Yes ☒ No

Have you ever been party to a Law Suit? ☐ Yes ☒ No   If yes, what type?

Any accidental bodily injury ever sustained requiring medical attention?
By you? ☒ Yes ☐ No   By your family? ☐ Yes ☐ No

If so, type of injury by you CAR   If so, type of injury by your family

Signature: Alexander Brown

⑮

JUROR NO.   316-17

BROWN, ALEXANDER

JUROR NO. 316-17   JUROR INFORMATION FORM   [PLEASE TYPE OR PRINT IN BLACK INK]

Single/Husband or Wife's Name	How long have you lived in County 4 YRS.	No. of Children 3	Phone No. 338-3333	Zip Code 72000	Your Age 34
ELLEN PYLE	Your present Employer W.K.M.	No. of years worked there ▼ 1		What is your type of work? MACHINE OPP.	
Your place of birth	Your Husband or Wife's Employer TEXAS INSTRUMENTS	No. of years worked there ▼ 8		What is their type of work? MAKING PARTS ELECTRIC	
HEARNE, WEST YORK					

Have you ever served on a Civil Jury? ☐ Yes ☒ No   Have you ever served on a Criminal Jury? ☐ Yes ☒ No

Have you ever been party to a Law Suit? ☐ Yes ☒ No   If yes, what type? THE ANSWER IS (NO)

Any accidental bodily injury ever sustained requiring medical attention?
By you? ☐ Yes ☒ No   By your family? ☐ Yes ☒ No

If so, type of injury by you FOOTBALL (COLAR BONE)   If so, type of injury by your family

Signature: Bill Everson Pyle

⑯

JUROR NO.   316-17

PYLE, BILL EVERSON

[Each potential juror completes an information form when summoned. Each attorney is given a photocopy of the completed set of juror forms to shorten voir dire examination. The potential jurors are seated in the "audience" portion of the courtroom in the same order as the numbers on their forms above.]

PLAINTIFF'S VOIR DIRE EXAMINATION OF PROSPECTIVE JURORS
(EXCERPT FROM TRANSCRIPT)

THE COURT: Good morning, ladies and gentlemen. You've been asked to come here this morning to serve as jurors in the case of Miranda Dominguez versus Scott's Food Stores, Inc. The Plaintiff is Ms. Dominguez, seated here at counsel table with her attorney, Mr. Elder. The Defendant, Scott's, is represented by Mr. Livingston, seated over here.

The attorneys have been given jury information forms which you have filled out, and they may have certain other questions to ask you. Listen to their questions carefully. They're not trying to pry into your personal life, they just want to get a fair and impartial jury. Mr. Elder, you may start your examination.

BY MR. ELDER:

[THE JURY SYSTEM; THE PARTICIPANTS.]   And I want to thank you, ladies and gentlemen, for being here and giving us of your valuable time to decide this case. You are performing a duty of citizenship, exercising a right that we cherish under our Constitution, and all I ask is that you fulfill that duty in the same way you would want it fulfilled if you were one of the parties to a lawsuit.

As the judge has told you, my name is Stephen Elder. My office is in the First Savings Building, 4 blocks over in that direction. I represent the lady you see sitting in front of you, Mrs. Dominguez. She is 63 years old and has lived in London for the past 20 years. I want to introduce you to her; Mrs. Dominguez, would you please stand up? Thank you. Now, having seen Mrs. Dominguez, and having met her this way, is there anyone who knows of any reason why they couldn't be absolutely fair in judging her case? (Silence.) I take it from your silence that the answer is no, and that all of you could be fair to Mrs. Dominguez.

Scott's Food Stores is represented by Mr. Bob Livingston, who is a partner in the firm of McIntosh & Walker. It is a large firm, with over 200 lawyers. What I need to ask you, is this: How many members of the jury panel know any lawyers with McIntosh & Walker, or have had any connection with the firm? (Several members of the panel respond by holding up their hands.)

Mr. Green, let me take you first. How do you know the name of the firm?

THE VENIREMAN: They once handled a lawsuit for a company I was involved in.

MR. ELDER: Well, from that experience, I assume you must have built up an acquaintance with some of their lawyers?

THE VENIREMAN: Yes, some.

MR. ELDER: Mr. Green, I'll ask you to search your mind carefully and tell us whether there is the slightest chance that your association with lawyers at McIntosh & Walker could affect you, even unconsciously, in listening just a little more carefully to what Mr. Livingston says, or whatever. Do you think you can guarantee me that it won't affect you? And more importantly (gesturing) can you guarantee to Mrs. Dominguez, as she sits here, that there won't be the slightest unconscious effect on you in this case?

THE VENIREMAN: Oh, of course, I would decide the case on the facts.

MR. ELDER: You are certain it could not possibly affect you in the slightest?

THE VENIREMAN: Yes.

MR. ELDER: Thank you, Mr. Green. (Pause.) Now, Mr. Brown, you also held up your hand.   [In this manner, Plaintiff's attorney speaks with each of the venirepersons who raise their hands.]

[PURPOSE OF THE EXAMINATION.] Before I go any farther, let me say this: we are in an introductory part of the trial now, that is designed to let you know something about the job you will be asked to do as potential jurors, and to let the attorneys know whether you, in your own mind, can think of anything that would keep you from being completely fair and impartial. If I ask a question that might apply to you--or even if I don't, but you know something that might affect you--please let me know about it.

By the way, you seem awfully quiet. Now is the time to speak up. Lawyers like juries that talk back. (Laughter.)

[THE CASE.] The type of case that you will hear about is called a "negligence" case. The evidence is going to show that Mrs. Dominguez went to a Scott's Food Store, Store No. 14, on Quitman Street, to do some shopping. The evidence will show you that she tried to get one of the baskets and took hold of the handle but the baskets were bent and defective, and that Mrs. Dominguez is an elderly lady, and when she pulled on the baskets in a normal manner, 5 or 6 baskets came out and ran over her . . . .

MR. LIVINGSTON: Excuse me. Your Honor, I object to counsel testifying and giving conclusions about what the evidence may or may not show, and to counsel giving a jury argument at this time.

THE COURT: Sustained.

MR. ELDER: It is our opinion that the Scott's Food Store was negligent in maintaining these baskets in this manner, and the complaint I have filed for Mrs. Dominguez says that this negligence consisted of maintaining the baskets in a bent and defective condition so that an elderly lady could not pull a single basket out without several coming out and running her over. Now, Mrs. Dominguez was caused to have a broken wrist and arm. The legal term for the type of damages we're talking about is "pain and suffering." I expect the evidence to show that the injury, and the discomfort, disability and permanent handicap Mrs. Dominguez has had and will have in the future are very great, and all of these things are part of what you are to consider as damages under pain and suffering. The Scott's people did not apologize, but filed an answer denying everything and saying that the accident was all Mrs. Dominguez's fault.

MR. LIVINGSTON: Objection, Your Honor.

THE COURT: Sustained.

MR. LIVINGSTON: I ask that the court instruct the jurors that they are to disregard these remarks of counsel.

THE COURT: The jurors will disregard these last remarks of counsel and not consider same for any purpose. All right, Mr. Elder, let's move along.

[OBTAINING COMMITMENTS FROM THE JURY.]

MR. ELDER: Is there anyone, who, for whatever reason, could not follow the law, which says that damages for pain and suffering are to be awarded as evidence warrants it? (Silence.) I take it from your silence that no one would be unable to make such an award. Now, let me ask this question, and this is important. If the evidence were to show that Scott's was in fact negligent, and if the evidence also were to show that Mrs. Dominguez sustained pain and suffering in a very great, very significant amount, is there anyone who could not find a corresponding great amount of damages for pain and suffering? (Silence.) I take it from your silence that everyone could do that.

What I'm getting at is this: Mrs. Dominguez is not here asking you for sympathy, but a part of her life has been taken away, and the law says that real damages are awardable--not just a pittance, but full compensation--and that's the way the law would apply to anyone here if you were injured, and I hope that doesn't happen!

58

[APPLICABLE LAW ON LIABILITY.] Now, I told you that this was a negligence case. One of the questions you will be asked at the end of the case is whether Scott's was "negligent." The judge will give you a definition of the term "negligence." I expect that he will use words something like this: "Negligence is the failure to use ordinary care, or the failure to use that degree of care that a person of ordinary prudence would exercise under the circumstances." In plain old ordinary language, negligence is simply carelessness. Is there anyone who would not be able to say Scott's was negligent, or in other words, careless, if the proof shows that it was? (Silence.)

I ask you to notice something else in the definition, too; the circumstances of the parties is one of the factors to be considered. Different standards of conduct may apply to one person than to another because of their circumstances. A child, say, or a grocery store owner, or an elderly lady are all in different positions. Is there anyone who would have any difficulty in judging Scott's and judging Mrs. Dominguez, under different standards, according to their circumstances? (Silence).

I believe the judge will tell you it's up to Mrs. Dominguez to bring in the initial evidence. I believe the judge will tell you that her burden is to prove her case by "a preponderance of the evidence." The word "preponderance" is just a fancy word for "the greater weight of the evidence." If you imagine the scales of justice (gesturing with arms), they might be exactly equal, or they may tip slightly, and that's the preponderance of the evidence. If the scales tip slightly, ever so slightly, in favor of Ms. Dominguez, it's your duty to render a verdict in her favor. Is there anyone who could not do that? (Silence.) Let me add that at the end of this case, I expect that you will find the case to be proved much more than slightly; we expect to bring you strong evidence. But that's the standard.

(At this point, Plaintiff similarly explained such terms as "proximate cause" and "ordinary care," and obtained commitments from the jurors to accept them.)

[POTENTIAL PREJUDICES.] As you all know, we are all victims of some degree of prejudice about almost everything. Sometimes that is all right, and sometimes it's even funny—we've all heard of Archie Bunker. But in a lawsuit, even small unconscious prejudices can be very harmful. Let me give you an example: Say a person might be injured in a bar. He might be injured by his own carelessness but on the other hand, he might be injured by the negligence of some other person. But you know what? A funny thing happens. We attorneys know that, in such a case, it would be extremely hard to win, just because the case happened in a bar. It's only natural. Now, I want to ask you about this case, and ask you to sincerely search the remotest parts of your unconscious, to see whether there's anything that might effect you in this case.

First, is there anyone who is prejudiced against the bringing of a lawsuit, just the fact of the suit itself? (Silence.) I take it from your silence that there is no one who feels that way, and I am glad because our system says that this is exactly what you should do when you are injured.

Now, I expect that it is possible that at the end of the case, you may think that I am not a polished or experienced lawyer. Mr. Livingston has a lot more experience in the courtroom than I do, because his practice is specialized in litigation, and I have a general practice, sort of like a family doctor as versus a specialist. I don't want the experience of the attorney to affect the outcome. Can all of you focus on the case itself, and disregard the experience of the attorneys? (Silence.)

Also, Mrs. Dominguez is a Mexican-American. She is, and has been, an American citizen since just after her birth, but frankly, she does not speak perfect English, and in fact she speaks English with a little bit of an accent. Now, as a Mexican-American, she actually shouldn't be subject to prejudice. She is the heir to a culture that is great and gracious. But I am sure you are all familiar with the problems that members of minority groups have in obtaining a fair trial. Is there anyone who would consciously or unconsciously hold it against her that she speaks English with the trace of an accent, or that she's Mexican-American? (Silence.)

Now, the law provides that a jury may find damages for pain and suffering without expert testimony, and in fact there is no scientific measure of these damages. The jury is the judge of that. We will show you medical records of the doctor who treated Mrs. Dominguez and hospital records that show her stays in the hospital and what happened there. Is there anyone who could not decide the case without the treating doctor actually being present?

A VENIREPERSON: Is there any reason why he couldn't be present?

MR. ELDER: Yes ma'am. Several reasons. I suppose the main reason is that Mrs. Dominguez would have to pay for his time, and she can't afford that. That would include his time spent waiting for court to open, like you and I had to do (Laughter.) But the main reason is that there's really no function the doctor would serve in determining pain and suffering, and the facts about the injury are all in the records. Can you accept evidence of that sort?

THE VENIREPERSON: Yes.

[CONCLUSION.] Ladies and gentlemen, thank you for your attention. I've watched you, and I've noticed that you've been attentive throughout this, and I've probably taken longer than I should. And I know those benches are hard. Sometimes I think they order the benches special, extra-hard benches, just for courtrooms. (Laughter.) But as Lady Godiva said when she got off the horse, I have come to my close. (Laughter.) Thanks, and Mr. Livingston will have a chance to visit with you now.

DEFENDANT'S VOIR DIRE EXAMINATION OF THE JURY (EXCERPT FROM TRANSCRIPT)

MR. LIVINGSTON: May it please the court; Mr. Elder, and ladies and gentlemen of the jury panel, I also want to thank you for being here.

[PREJUDICES.] Mr. Elder has talked about the kind of prejudices that can affect us in a lawsuit, and I agree. One of the things that sometimes affects us very subtly is when the Defendant is a company or corporation. Is there anyone who feels that a corporation, like Scott's Food Stores in this case, ought to be dealt with more strictly than an individual? The law says that Scott's Foods has the same legal rights in a suit like this as any other person. Is there anyone who would have a tendency to decide that Scott's ought to pay a higher amount of damage just because it's a company? (Silence.) I take it from your silence that no one would. There's a natural human tendency to say to yourself, well, this is a large company, and it must be rich, although with the price squeeze I hear grocers are in these days I'm not too sure that's true.

I expect that one of the instructions the judge will give you is that passion, prejudice, sympathy, or bias is to play no part in your deliberations. That is just another way of saying that you should not let yourself decide against Scott's Food Store, or in favor of Mrs. Dominguez, just because you have sympathy for her or passion against the Store.

60

In that connection, does anyone know of any reason why you would be motivated by any prejudice against Scott's Foods? Occasionally, people are dissatisfied with merchandise they bought, or with an individual in the company that they dealt with. I take it from you silence that there is no one that feels that way.

[LAYING THE BASIS FOR CHALLENGES FOR CAUSE.] Now, I see that several people on the jury panel have had previous instances to be injured yourself. If you serve on the jury it will be your task to set these matters out of your mind completely. Is there anyone who might tend to identify with the plaintiff because of a previous injury you yourself have had?

A VENIREPERSON: I'm sitting here thinking about it, and I had a broken arm once and my insurance didn't cover it.

MR. LIVINGSTON: Would you be able to assure us and guarantee us, that you could decide the case without thinking about your own experience at all? Could you put it completely out of your mind?

THE VENIREPERSON: I would try, and that's all I can do.

DEFENDANT'S ATTORNEY: I don't mean to pressure you, but you're the only one who would know. Your Honor, I wonder if we might be allowed to approach the bench? Ma'am, I apologize for singling you out. Don't be embarrassed, but I wonder if you would mind approaching the judge with us? (Both attorneys and the Venireperson approached the bench, whereupon the following proceedings occurred:) Now, Ms. Delorme, unless you are a very unusual person, it would be natural for it to be impossible for you to really guarantee us that you can decide this case without sympathy for someone who may have been in a situation similar to you, such as Mrs. Dominguez.

THE VENIREPERSON: Yes, sir. I can't say.

MR. LIVINGSTON: Did the experience of your injury leave you with a bad taste in your mouth, or did it leave you with a fixed opinion against the way our system goes about compensating or not compensating people who have been injured?

THE VENIREPERSON: It sure did.

MR. LIVINGSTON: And don't feel shy at all about telling us this -- you would have to tell us that that fixed opinion would tend to be in your mind throughout the case, and to affect you toward sympathy for the injured person.

THE VENIREPERSON: Well, frankly, yes.

MR. LIVINGSTON: I challenge for cause.

MR. ELDER: Just a moment. Mrs. Delorme, you are not telling this court that before even hearing the evidence, you have a fixed opinion that Scott's Foods is guilty of negligence, or that Mrs. Dominguez should recover anything? You're not saying you wouldn't decide the case on all the evidence, and decide it fairly?

THE VENIREPERSON: Oh, no. I would have to hear all the evidence and I would be fair.

THE COURT: I think we better excuse this lady. (To the venireperson): If you need a slip for your employer, the clerk will fix you up.

THE VENIREPERSON: I can go?

MR. LIVINGSTON: (again addressing the panel): Ladies and gentlemen, it's not unusual for our personal experiences to affect us, and Mrs. Delorme has just done exactly what a person who's forthright ought to do in such a situation. Is there anyone else who has the least question about their ability to serve as jurors and be completely fair to both sides? (This questioning resulted in the successful challenge for cause of one additional venireperson.)

[THE PLAINTIFF'S BURDEN OF PROOF.] Now, Mrs. Dominguez claims in her complaint that Scott's was guilty of an act of negligence. She claims that she was not careless at all. She claims that she was injured in the sum of at least twenty-five thousand dollars. It is our contention, and I think you will agree when you see this case, that that sum is vastly inflated. And, although Mrs. Dominguez did have a broken wrist, our answer is that Scott's was not guilty of negligence at all, but just did what an ordinary grocer would have done in conducting its business.

I am sure you are aware that this courthouse is always open for business. Anyone can sue anyone else for any amount, just by filing a complaint. Someone can sue me, or you, on a claim that may or may not be valid, and bring us into court, and they don't have to make any kind of proof or pass any screening test in order to file. They just file suit. It ultimately depends on you ladies and gentlemen to separate the wheat from the chaff. That is why it's up to the Plaintiff to prove her case, before they reach into the pocket of someone else and take twenty-five thousand dollars, or any amount, from whoever they sue. Is there anyone who disagrees with the law that says that plaintiff must prove her case by the preponderance of the evidence before she can require Scott's, or anyone else, to pay her?

[THE LAW OF LIABILITY: NEGLIGENCE AND CONTRIBUTORY NEGLIGENCE.] As Mr. Elder has told you, the judge will probably define the term "negligence" by using the term "ordinary care." Incidentally, the word "carelessness" doesn't figure into it at all. I expect the judge will tell you that ordinary care is that care that an ordinary grocer would use under the circumstances. Basically, before you find that Scott's Foods was guilty of negligence, you must find that it is guilty of some kind of unreasonable act, that an ordinary grocer would not do. If you do not find that, you should not find Scott's Foods guilty of negligence. Is there anyone who disagrees with that principle?

Further, the law says that Mrs. Dominguez is responsible to exercise reasonable care for her own safety. Now, Mrs. Dominguez is an attractive, nice lady. At the end of the case, I don't expect that you will dislike her; in fact, I expect you might find her a likeable lady. However, notwithstanding that, if she wasn't careful about her own safety, it's your duty to say so. Is there anyone who would have any difficulty in saying that? (Silence.) I take it from your silence that no one would have difficulty, and that you would do so if the evidence shows that to be the case.

(At this point, Defendant's attorney covered several other principles: for example, he pointed out that since the Plaintiff goes first, jurors will have to wait to hear both sides of the story; that part of a lawyer's job is to object when he thinks the other side is violating the rules, and that the jurors should not hold it against his client if he found it necessary to object; that it is the jurors' job to judge the credibility of the witnesses, and that there are several factors to be used in judging credibility—hope of gain by plaintiff, prior inconsistent statements (such as might be found in depositions), and the like. He also questioned jurors about prior injuries, serious illnesses, financial difficulties, and other factors that might be the basis of sympathy or prejudice.)

MR. LIVINGSTON: Ladies and gentlemen, thank you for your attention. That's all the questions I have. I know you've been hearded around today and rounded up kind of like cattle, and I've tried to be as quick as I could. Thanks again.

THE COURT: All right. Make your strikes, gentlemen.

PLAINTIFF'S JURY LIST AND CHALLENGES

1 TAYLOR, ALICE LOUISE
2 MARBURY, RALPH
3 GUNTHER, LYLE K.
4 WALSTON, CLARA JANE
5 SCOTT, VERA MRS.
6 ~~GOEDECKE, J M III~~
7 TILLMAN, JENARA LEE
8 McIVER, MARY
9 ~~GREEN, ROBERT WAYNE~~
10 FLORENCE, JOHN A.
11 DELORME, ELAINE — cause
12 TYLER, JENNIE C. — cause
13 ~~MAGNUSSON, WILLIAM P.~~
14 CORTELLI, PHILIP R.
15 BROWN, ALEXANDER — alternate
16 PYLE, BILL EVERSON — alternate

DEFENDANT'S JURY LIST AND CHALLENGES

1 ~~TAYLOR, ALICE LOUISE~~
2 MARBURY, RALPH
3 ~~GUNTHER, LYLE K.~~
4 WALSTON, CLARA JANE
5 SCOTT, VERA MRS.
6 GOEDECKE, J M III
7 TILLMAN, JENARA LEE
8 McIVER, MARY
9 GREEN, ROBERT WAYNE
10 ~~FLORENCE, JOHN A.~~
11 DELORME, ELAINE — cause
12 TYLER, JENNIE C. — cause
13 MAGNUSSON, WILLIAM P.
14 CORTELLI, PHILIP R.
15 BROWN, ALEXANDER — alternate
16 PYLE, BILL EVERSON — alternate

CLERK'S FINAL JURY LIST

MARBURY, RALPH
WALSTON, CLARA JANE
SCOTT, VERA MRS.
TILLMAN, JENARA LEE
McIVER, MARY
CORTELLI, PHILIP R.

B. NOTES AND QUESTIONS REGARDING JURY SELECTION

1. ATTORNEY'S GOALS AND TACTICS IN VOIR DIRE EXAMINATION. When examination of the venire is conducted by attorneys, strategic considerations dominate. Attorneys may engage in some or all of the following behaviors: (a) asking questions to find out about disqualifications or orientations of jurors (the most obvious, and most ostensibly proper, purpose); (b) giving jurors a selective preview of the

evidence; (c) defining legal terms in a favorable manner ("negligence is carelessness" for plaintiff; negligence means "my client must be guilty of an unreasonable act" by defendant); (d) building rapport or injecting prejudice ("I'm a family practitioner and the opposing firm has 200 lawyers"); (e) injecting inadmissible evidence (e.g., dwelling heavily upon panel members' insurance connections, suggestively); (f) conditioning jurors to accept proof ("is there anyone who would hesitate at awarding 2 million dollars in damages if the evidence shows that sum to be proper?") There are many other purposes for which attorneys use the voir dire process—some ethical, some marginal, and some flatly improper. Incidentally, there are few guidelines governing proper examination, and much is left to the discretion of the judge.

2. "LABEL" CHARACTERISTICS V. "INDIVIDUAL" CHARACTERISTICS. The venire are required to fill out "juror information forms" that give certain unambigious or "label" information about them. These forms shorten the voir dire examination because they provide standard information. Most attorneys wish, also, to examine jurors verbally, to get the "feel" of each venireperson. Consider this question: Which is likely to be a better predictor of the attorney's peremptory challenges—the "label" characteristics or the "individual" characteristics?

If you have answered that "individual" characteristics—the individual "feel" of the juror—ought to be more important, your thoughts are noble. But consider the following: Plaintiff's strikes were carbon copies of each other on "label" characteristics. All are managerial or professional, all are caucasian anglo males, virtually all are middle-aged, all are educated, all are married, most have families, and virtually all reside in suburbs. Plaintiff would probably accept law students—but strike lawyers. Plaintiff's lawyer has exercised his challenges by "labels." Maybe the difficulty of obtaining reliable information by "individual" inquiry within the time reasonably allotted to jury selection necessitates the use of gross characteristics.

3. PEREMPTORY CHALLENGES. 28 U.S.C. sec. 1870 states that in civil cases, "each party shall be entitled to three peremptory challenges." In multiple party cases, the court "may allow additional peremptory challenges."

4. CHALLENGES FOR CAUSE. Notice that Defendant has obtained the removal of two potential jurors for cause. The questioning of jurors for this purpose is, again, an art form: The juror must be induced to make statements showing a bias or prejudice that cannot be set aside. A typical technique is to appeal to the juror's integrity and make forthrightness appear commendable. For strategy reasons, attorneys usually identify jurors they wish to remove and then initiate the process of obtaining responses leading to disqualification.

5. EXAMINATION BY JUDGE OR ATTORNEYS? Arguably, examination by attorneys begins the trial with a showboating personality contest that detracts from the determination of the case by law and evidence. On the other hand, examination by the judge is rarely as vigorous, informed, or likely to ferret out prejudice as examination by the attorneys. Which is preferable? Note that Rule 47(a) grants the court considerable discretion, and the most common practice in federal courts is for the court itself to conduct the examination and to receive written suggestions of questions from the attorneys.

C. THE TRIAL: PLAINTIFF'S EVIDENCE

TRANSCRIPT OF THE PROCEEDINGS

BE IT REMEMBERED that upon the trial of the above numbered and entitled cause, which was commenced on the 18th day of September, A.D. 2000, in said

Court before the Honorable John T. Hughes, United States District Judge Presiding, and a jury, the following evidence was adduced and proceedings had:

MR. LIVINGSTON: We would invoke the Rule, your honor.

THE COURT: All witnesses please rise and be sworn. (After swearing the witnesses): The rule has been invoked. You must remain outside, and out of the hearing of the evidence, and you are not to discuss the testimony in this case with anyone, except that you may discuss it with the attorneys for either side in the case.

EDWARD DOMINGUEZ
first having been duly sworn, in response to questions propounded to him, testified as follows:

DIRECT EXAMINATION (EXCERPT FROM TRANSCRIPT)

BY MR. ELDER:
Q Would you please state your name to the jury?
A Edward Dominguez.
Q You will have to speak up, Mr. Dominguez, so that all the members of the jury can understand you.
A Edward Dominguez. That is my name.
Q Where do you live, Mr. Dominguez.
A I live on 2944 Dunham. D-u-n-h-a-m.
Q Is that a street here in London?
A Yes.
Q Do you work?
A Yes.
Q What is your employment? Tell the jury what your employment is.
A I am a floor sander and finisher.
Q Who do you work for?
A William's Floor Company.
Q How long have you been working for the William's Floor Company?
A Thirteen years.
Q Thirteen years. What sort of work do you do? Floor sanding--is that with a machine you operate?
A Yes.
Q Do you know the Plaintiff in this lawsuit, Miranda Dominguez?
A Yes.
Q Would you tell the jury how you happen to know her?
A Well, I took her to the store.
Q What is your relationship to Ms. Dominguez?
A Oh! I am her husband.
Q And how long have you been married to Ms. Dominguez?
A Since '71.
Q Since 1971. That is about twenty-nine years?
A Yes.
Q Do you have any children?
A One daughter.
Q You have one daughter. Tell the jury what is the daughter's name?
A Thelma Rodriguez.
Q Does she live in London also?
A Yes.
Q Mr. Dominguez, you know that this day is the trial of a lawsuit?
A Yes.

Q And you know that this lawsuit grows out of the accident that your wife had?
A Yes.
Q And do you recall when it was that your wife had this accident that is the basis of this lawsuit?
A I forget the year, about four years ago. It was about 5:30 in the evening.
Q Do you remember the day of the week?
A No.
Q Do you remember the time of the day that this happened?
A About 5:30.
Q Had you gone to work that day?
A I had gotten off from work.
Q After you got off work, did you go home?
A Yes.
Q Then after you went home from work did you and your wife do anything?
A I took her to the store.
Q What store did you take her to?
A The old store that used to be on Quitman.
Q Whose store is that?
A Scott's No. 14.
Q It has a big sign out front that says Scott's, is that right?
A Yes.
Q When you took her to this store did you take her in the car?
A Yes.
Q What kind of car was it?
A A Chevrolet.
Q And did you go in the store with her?
A No. I stayed in the car.
Q Why did you stay in the car?
A Because I always stay in the car and she goes in and then I go help her out with the groceries.
Q Had you been in that store before?
A Yes.
Q And did they have some shopping carts, the carts with the baskets on them?
A Yes, they had baskets.
Q You pulled up in front of the store and she went in the store by herself, is that correct?
A Yes, she always did.
Q What was the next thing that happened?
A It was not long until a lady came running out and said my wife had fallen down.
Q About how much time elapsed before you found out something might be wrong?
A The lady came and told me. I had not been there hardly no time when the lady came.
Q Did you know this lady that came out of the store?
A No. I did not notice who it was.
Q But after this lady came out what did you do?
A I went running inside.
Q You ran inside the store. Which door did you run in?
A The same one she went in.
Q Did you see you wife when you got inside the store?
A She was there and the assistant manager got her a box to sit on.
Q Was that a box that groceries might have come in or do you know?
A I don't remember what it was. I just picked her up.
Q Now, tell the jury whether there were any people around when you came in.
A Yes, and the assistant manager was there.
Q You say the assistant manager was there. Now, how do you know that this was

the assistant manager?

A Because he had assistant manager on his--the manager was not there at the time, it was the assistant manager.

Q And did your wife speak to you?

A Yes, she was crying. She said she was hurting pretty much.

Q What complaint did she make? What injury did she complain of?

A Her hand.

Q Which hand is that?

A The right hand.

Q Did you look at her right hand?

A Yes.

Q Tell the jury what kind of injury it was and how it appeared to be hurt.

A Her hand was broken. She fell on her hand.

Q Was it distorted any or off to the side or anything like this?

A Yes. It was.

Q Did you have any conversation about how she got her hand hurt or did you concentrate on other matters?

A She just said that she pulled one of those baskets and she fell down.

Q Did you do anything?

A Yes. I took her to the hospital.

Q What hospital did you take her to?

A County Memorial Downtown.

Q Was this the closest hospital to the location where you were?

A Yes.

Q Now, I believe that your wife had been in that hospital before, hadn't she?

A Yes.

Q And she had been under the care of a doctor that specializes in bone breaks and that sort of thing, hadn't she?

A Yes.

Q And who is that doctor?

A Dr. Ellman.

Q This time did you have Dr. Ellman called? Did you tell the people at the hospital to call Dr. Ellman?

A Yes.

Q Mr. Dominguez, did Dr. Ellman come to the hospital?

A Yes. He did.

Q What time do you think it was when you arrived at the hospital, you and your wife?

A About 6:00, around 6:00.

Q Was she in one of those side rooms off the emergency room of that hospital?

A Yes.

Q Was there any conversation when the doctor arrived?

A Yes. He said--

Q Just a minute. As the result of that conversation did the doctor make an examination of your wife?

A Yes.

Q And what did the examination focus on?

MR. LIVINGSTON: Excuse me. Your Honor, we object to this---

A Broken arm and broken hand.

MR. ELDER: I withdraw the question.

THE COURT: If an attorney stands up to make an objection, stop talking until the Court has had a chance to rule on the objection.

67

Q Did you see the doctor actually do anything to your wife? Not what was said, but did he actually do anything while you were there in the treatment room or emergency room?
A Oh, yes.
Q What did the doctor actually do while you were in his presence. Tell the jury.
A He worked on her hand, wrapped her up with bandages.
Q What else did he do?
A He put her in the hospital that night.
Q How long did you stay at the hospital?
A I stayed there until about 1:00 o'clock in the morning.
Q Did the doctor put a cast on your wife's arm that night?
A Yes.
Q And did she get out of the hospital later on?
A She got out the next day.
Q She got out of the hospital the next day. She had a cast on her arm, is that right?
A Yes.
Q Did she go home when you took her out of the hospital? Did you take her home?
A Yes. I took her home.
Q When you got home did she complain to you of any pain?
A Yes. She kept complaining.
Q Did she take any medication?
A No.
Q She never took any medication? She never took any pills or anything?
A Oh, yes. The doctor gave her some and she took those pills.
Q How long did she have a cast on her arm?
A I don't remember---pretty long time---pretty long time.
Q Was it more than two weeks?
A Yes, it was more than two months.
Q Then did the doctor take the cast off later?
A Yes.
Q Was your wife completely recovered when the doctor took the cast off?

   MR. LIVINGSTON: Excuse me. Your Honor, we object to that as calling for a conclusion on the part of this witness.

   MR. ELDER: I withdraw the question and I will rephrase it.

Q After the doctor took the cast off did you wife ever complain of any other discomfort in her wrist?
A Yes.
Q As the result of that did you ever take her to the doctor's office?
A Yes.
Q While you were at the doctor's office did you ever see the doctor do anything by way of treatment for her?
A I did not go in. I just took her.
Q Do you know of your own knowledge, Mr. Dominguez, as to whether or not the doctor admitted her into the hospital later?
A He admitted her to the hospital.
Q Which hospital was that?
A The same, Memorial.
Q The second time how long was she in the hospital?
A I think it was two weeks.
Q She was in the hospital two weeks. Did she have a cast on her arm when she got out of the hospital? Tell the jury whether she had a cast on her arm when she got out of the hospital?

A I believe she did. I do not remember.

Q You are not sure whether she had a cast on. Are you able to tell us how long she had the cast on after she got out of the hospital?

A About two months I believe.

Q Later on this cast came off too, is that right?

A Right.

Q Did Dr. Ellman take that cast off?

A Yes.

Q And afterward did you ever take your wife back to see Dr. Ellman after the second cast was removed from her arm?

A Yes. Many times.

Q Approximately how many times did you take her back to see the doctor?

A I took her many times and then this lady started taking her. She started taking her because I had to miss work. This lady took her to the doctor.

Q What is her name?

A Her name is Tina. I do not remember her last name. She is a friend of my wife.

Q How long after the cast came off was your wife under the doctor's care?

A She went on for about a year after that.

Q That was in 1997?

A Yes.

Q How long was it after this accident before she was able to use her hand well?

A Well, she still don't use it well.

Q How long was it before it seemed like she was getting the use of it back?

A A year and a half or two.

Q Your wife was injured before this accident on another time, wasn't she?

A Yes.

Q Tell the jury when she got hurt before?

A I don't remember.

Q Was it more than two or three years before this accident?

A I don't remember.

Q Do you remember what part of the body she injured?

A No. I think it was a leg this time, I believe.

Q I believe that also happened to be in a Scott's store at that time?

A Yes.

Q She recovered from the injury that she got before?

A Yes.

Q Was she hospitalized as a result of the injury she sustained several years before this accident happened?

A She went to a doctor.

Q Now, Mr. Dominguez, I believe you have testified that you had been in this grocery store before the accident happened?

A Me?

Q Yes.

A Yes, many a time.

Q How long had that grocery store been there to your knowledge.

A I don't know.

Q How long had you been living in the neighborhood? Tell the jury how long you had lived in the neighborhood where this grocery store was.

A Twenty-six years.

Q In the same neighborhood?

A Yes, and the store was there then.

Q The store had been there all the time that you were there as you recall?

A Yes.

Q So would it be fair to say this is an old store?

A It was old. They tore it down.

69

Q Mr. Dominguez, did you ever have occasion to--you did go inside more than just to help your wife out with the groceries, did you ever go inside and take shopping carts?
A Oh, yes.
Q And you have done some grocery shopping yourself?
A Yes.
Q And pushed your grocery cart up and down the aisle?
A Yes.
Q Now, Mr. Dominguez, did you ever have occasion to make any observation of the state of repair of these shopping carts? Did you notice the condition they were in?
A There were some of them that---

   MR. LIVINGSTON: Your Honor, we object to the witness' answer as not being responsive to the question. He was asked whether he made any observation as to their condition which would require a yes or no answer.

Q Mr. Dominguez, this question has a yes or no answer. Did you ever make any observation about the condition of the shopping carts?
A Yes.
Q Tell the jury what condition they were in.

   MR. LIVINGSTON: Your Honor, we would object to any questions by Counsel relative to carts at other times and move the Court that the only relevant testimony would be on the occasion in question.

   THE COURT: You may rephrase your question.

BY MR. ELDER:
Q Had you ever seen new carts being brought into this store?
A No, I never have.
Q So the carts that were there before---did you make any observation---this question has a yes or no answer---did you make an observation about the state of repair of those carts?
A Yes.
Q Tell the jury what condition they were in.

   MR. LIVINGSTON: We object to that as being irrelevant and immaterial to this matter.

   THE COURT: Sustained.

Q Did you ever see carts left out in the parking lot?
A Oh, yes.
Q Did you ever see any carts that were used by people to carry groceries home as they walked home?
A Yes.
Q Did you ever see them left out in the rain?
A Yes.
Q Did you ever see them lying on their sides?
A Yes.
Q Have you ever seen children playing in the carts?
A Yes, many times.
Q Now, you did not go up and inspect the cart or carts that your wife might have been pushed down by?
A No.

Q How old are you, Mr. Dominguez?
A Sixty-four.
Q How old is your wife?
A Sixty-two.
Q How old was she at the time of this accident?
A She was sixty, but she is sixty-three now.

MR. ELDER: Pass the witness.

CROSS EXAMINATION (EXCERPT FROM TRANSCRIPT)

BY MR. LIVINGSTON:
Q Mr. Dominguez, your wife has been a housewife for twenty or thirty years, is this correct?
A Yes.
Q She was not employed and has not been employed in many many years, is this correct?
A Yes.

MR. LIVINGSTON: I do not have any further questions, Your Honor.

REDIRECT EXAMINATION (EXCERPT FROM TRANSCRIPT)

BY MR. ELDER:
Q Now, your wife has not worked outside the home, but tell the jury whether or not she was doing her housework and homework?
A Yes. She did her housework.
Q Tell the jury whether or not after the accident she was able to maintain her housework duties as a housewife?
A No, she was not able.
Q What was she not able to do?
A Nothing.
Q Well, specifically tell the jury what she could not do after the accident that she could do before the accident?
A She could do everything before and afterwards she couldn't do nothing.
Q Did she ever have to get anybody to help her after the accident?
A Yes.
Q What sort of help did she receive?
A Helped clean the house.
Q Who would help her?
A Friends.
Q Did you ever help?
A Me?
Q Yes.
A Sure I helped.
Q What did you do?
A I would help her.
Q What sort of work? What sort of jobs did you do?
A I cooked and I washed and everything. Mopping.
Q Did you ever do any scrubbing?
A Yes.
Q You did the cooking?
A I did it all.
Q And over what period of time did this last?
A How long?
Q Yes. How long did you do it after the accident?

A Two years.
Q Who else would help her?
A This friend of hers. The one that took her to the doctor.
Q Did your wife ever have any exercises or any therapy or any treatment that she took at home after she got out of the hospital?
A No, I don't think she did.
Q Did she ever bathe her hand or do anything like that?
A Oh, yes.
Q What sort of activity was this?
A She would soak her hand in water.
Q How long would she do that, Mr. Dominguez?
A I don't know.
Q Was it more than two or three months?
A Yes.

    MR. ELDER: Pass the witness, Your Honor.

    MR. LIVINGSTON: No questions, Your Honor.

    THE COURT: You may step down.

    MR. LIVINGSTON: Your Honor, this witness is still under the rule. He is not a party to the lawsuit.

    THE COURT: Aproach the bench, please.

(Conference at the bench.)

    MR. ELDER: Mr. Dominguez, you are going to have to step outside.

THELMA RODRIGUEZ
    first having been duly sworn, in response to questions propounded to her, testified as follows:

DIRECT EXAMINATION (EXCERPT FROM TRANSCRIPT)

BY MR. ELDER:
Q Would you state your name for the jury, please?
A Thelma Rodriguez.
Q Is it Mrs.?
A Mrs.
    * * *
Q Do you know the Plaintiff in this lawsuit, Ms. Miranda Dominguez?
A She is my mother.
Q Do you have any brothers or sisters?
A None.

[Ms. Rodriguez testifies that she is married to Lupe Rodriguez, has lived in London all her life, has one child, and is not now working but worked until one week ago at an employment agency in the Chamber of Commerce Building. Before the accident, Ms. Rodriguez states, she lived near her mother and visited with her occasionally.]

Q And did she ever complain to you of any injury or illness?
A No.
Q Did she seem to be able to do her housework?

A Yes. Always.

Q And to do the regular activities that a woman of her age who is the only person who does the work in her house, is that right?

A Yes.

Q Do you recall when your mother got hurt?

A In the middle of May when she fell.

Q What year?

A 1996.

    * * *

Q You were not present when she fell?

A No. I was not.

Q Did you see your mother after the accident?

A The very next day I went to the hospital to see her in the morning.

    * * *

Q Did you ever go to the grocery store?

A Yes.

    * * *

Q So when you went to the grocery store afterward, approximately how long after the accident did you have occasion to go to the grocery store?

A One week or a week and a half.

Q Was there any new equipment in the grocery store?

A Not that I remember. No.

Q Did you make an observation about the state of repair of the shopping baskets?

A Yes.

Q Would you tell the jury what was the condition of the baskets when you went in?

    MR. LIVINGSTON: Excuse me. Your Honor, may I take the witness on voir dire for a moment?

    THE COURT: All right.

VOIR DIRE EXAMINATION (EXCERPT FROM TRANSCRIPT)

BY MR. LIVINGSTON:

Q It is my understanding that what he is asking you now about is several weeks after the accident. Is this your understanding?

A I really don't know how long after the accident or if it was before the accident. I know we shopped there on our way home.

Q It could have been any time period within several months one way or the other?

A It was not several months because we shopped at least once a week or maybe twice.

    MR. LIVINGSTON: Your Honor, again we object to this as being irrelevant and immaterial to any issue involved in this particular case.

    THE COURT: Sustained.

DIRECT EXAMINATION CONTINUED (EXCERPT FROM TRANSCRIPT)

BY MR. ELDER:

Q Will you tell the jury whether your mother complained of any injury after she got released from the hospital?

A Yes. She did.

Q What injury did she complain of?

A Her wrist.

Q   After the cast was removed did she ever complain to you of any further dis-
    comfort with her right wrist?
A   Yes.
Q   And what was the complaint?
A   I did not see it before the cast was put on it but it looked worse, I think,
    when the cast was removed. It was very swollen and she was going through
    quite a bit of pain.
Q   Do you know of your own knowledge whether she went in the hospital again?
A   Yes.
Q   And when she went in the hospital was another cast put on her wrist?
A   I don't think so. I don't remember.
Q   How long did she stay in the hospital?
A   About two weeks.
Q   After she was released from the hospital did she fully recover?
A   No.
Q   What was she unable to do after she was released from the hospital that she
    was able to do before?
A   Well, she could not do anything like she did before as far as her housework
    or anything, anything that she had to do for her personal self.
Q   How did she manage with the housework?
A   My father had to go home and do it because I could not.
Q   Why couldn't you do it?

[The witness states that she could not help her mother because "I was having a baby." Friends would
come in to help, but they could not afford to hire anyone to help. The witness did not take her mother to
the doctor because "I do not drive," and doesn't know how long her mother went to the doctor: "possibly two, three or four months." She testifies that her mother was injured in the same store several years
before, and it was "a leg injury but I really don't remember."]

        MR. ELDER: Pass the witness.

CROSS EXAMINATION (EXCERPT FROM TRANSCRIPT)

BY MR. LIVINGSTON:
Q   Mrs. Rodriguez, is Mrs. Martinez a close friend of your mother's?
A   Yes, a friend of my mother's for twenty years.

        MR. LIVINGSTON: Pass the witness.

        MR. ELDER: No further questions of this witness, Your Honor. If the Court
please, at this time we would ask that the materials which have been previously
identified and admitted into evidence may be passed among the jury.

        THE COURT: All right. You are excused.

        MR. ELDER: We would call the Plaintiff, Ms. Dominguez.

        Ms. MIRANDA DOMINGUEZ
        first having been duly sworn, in response to questions propounded to her,
testified as follows:

DIRECT EXAMINATION (EXCERPT FROM TRANSCRIPT)

BY MR. ELDER:

(In a manner similar to his questioning of Mr. Dominguez, Mr. Elder estabishes Ms. Dominguez's background. She lives at 2944 Dunham, a house she and her husband rent. Before living there, the Dominguezes lived six years on Southmore Street. She identifies herself as the wife of Edward Dominguez and the mother of Thelma Rodriguez.)

Q Ms. Dominguez, can you tell the jury when this lawsuit happened?
A It was in 1996 on May 7th. I walked in the store---
Q (Interrupting.) Ms. Dominguez, I am going to ask you to just answer the question I ask. Okay?
A Okay, sir.
   * * *
Q Ms. Dominguez, had your husband gone to work that day?
A Yes.
Q What time, if you remember, had he returned from work?
A He came home about 5:00 o'clock and I told him I need a few items.
Q Ms. Dominguez, I am going to ask you to just answer the question that I ask.
A Okay.
Q And as a result of your conversation did you go any place?
A No, sir, just to the store. That is all.
Q What store did you go to?
A Scott's No. 14.
Q Had you been to that store before?
A Yes.
Q Had that store been there a long time as you recall?
A Yes.
Q How many years had that store been there?
A Oh, about twenty or twenty-four.
Q Had there been any rebuilding of the store?
A Not until two or three years ago they built a new building.
Q Had you in your visits to the store ever seen them make any repairs or improvements in the store?
A No.

   MR. LIVINGSTON: We object to this as being irrelevant and immaterial.

   THE COURT: Sustained.

Q When you shopped at this store before, Ms. Dominguez, would you tell the members of this jury how you carried your groceries around?
A Well, I carried them in the basket but sometimes the baskets---
Q (Interrupting.) Ms. Dominguez, I ask you to just answer the questions that I ask you. You say that you carry them in the basket. Do you mean the shopping cart baskets on wheels?
A Yes.
Q Had you ever had any difficulty with the shopping carts on wheels?
A Yes, I did.

   MR. LIVINGSTON: Excuse me. Your Honor, we would object to this as being irrelevant and immaterial and not tied to any time period.

   THE COURT: Sustained.

Q During the period immediately prior to your visit on the day that you were injured on the 7th of May---when was the last time you had been in the store before you got injured?

A   A week before.
Q   About a week before?
A   Yes, sir.
Q   At that time had you had any difficulty operating the shopping carts?

      MR. LIVINGSTON: Excuse me. Your Honor, we object to that as being irrelevant and immaterial.

      THE COURT: Sustained.

Q   At the time you were in the store on the day that you were injured, Ms. Dominguez, did you make any observation about the shopping carts?
A   No.
Q   Did you notice whether any of them were---did you notice anything about the state of repair about the---

      MR. LIVINGSTON: Your Honor, we object to that. The witness has already answered the question and we object to Counsel leading his witness after she has answered the question in the negative.

      THE COURT: I have not heard the question yet.

      MR. LIVINGSTON: Sir?

      THE COURT: He did not finish his question.

      MR. LIVINGSTON: I apologize to the Court. I did not mean to cut him off.

Q   Did you make any observation about the condition of the shopping carts when you were in there?

      MR. LIVINGSTON: Objection, Your Honor. She has already answered the question. It is repetitious. The question was answered immediately prior to the question framed by counsel.

      THE COURT: Overruled.

Q   Go ahead and answer the question, please.
A   Well, I never had seen the baskets being repaired or nothing.

      MR. LIVINGSTON: Your Honor, we object to that as not being responsive.

      THE COURT: Sustained.

Q   I am not asking you whether you ever saw them repaired, I am asking you, did you see the condition of them when you went into the store?
A   Yes. They looked pretty old already.
Q   Did any of them appear rusty?
A   Yes.
Q   Did any of them appear to be bent?
A   Yes, sir.
Q   Did any of the wheels ever not turn or would not go straight?

      MR. LIVINGSTON: Excuse me. Your Honor, we object if Counsel is speaking of any other day other than May 7, 1996.

THE COURT: Sustained.

MR. ELDER: We withdraw the question.

Q Did you ever notice that any of the tubular frames were bent on this day?
A No. I did not notice that.
Q Now, you had been there before, hadn't you?
A Yes, sir.
Q And had you ever had difficulty previously?
A Yes. I did.

MR. LIVINGSTON: Excuse me. Your Honor, we object to that as being totally irrelevant and immaterial.

THE COURT: Sustained.

MR. ELDER: I did not finish the question. Are you objecting to her answer or my unfinished question?

Q Ms. Dominguez, did you have in your mind any feeling of danger about these carts?
A I did once.
Q At this time, on this day of May 7th, you did not feel that they were danger-ous, did you?
A No.
Q Will you tell the jury in your own words, Ms. Dominguez, whether anything unusual happened when you went in the store?
A Well, I walked in the store and I went inside to get my basket to do some shopping.
* * *
Q Ms. Dominguez, were these baskets stacked up?
A Yes, sir. They were all stuck together.
Q The baskets inside each other?
A Yes.
Q And I believe that the back of the basket facing you flips up and the other basket moves in behind it, is that right?
A That is right.

MR. LIVINGSTON: Your Honor, I would object to Counsel leading his witness.

THE COURT: Don't lead your witness.

Q So you walked up to a row of baskets?
A That is right.
Q What, if anything, happened then?
* * *
A Well, I got hold with my right hand to pull the basket and the whole basket went into me---
Q (Interrupting.) Now, Ms. Dominguez, you are going to have to speak very slowly. Please move the microphone up so that the jury can understand what happened.
A I went inside to get the basket with my right hand and the whole row of bas-kets came toward me and I fell down on my right hand but I did not notice that my hand was broken until the manager---
* * *
Q So when several baskets cam toward you what, if anything, happened?

MR. LIVINGSTON: Your Honor, we object to Counsel testifying and we object to his leading his witness.

THE COURT: Sustained.

Q As the baskets came toward you what, if anything, happened?
A I fell on the floor with my right hand.
Q Pardon?
A I fell on the floor with my right hand broken.
Q How did you fall down?
A Because the baskets pushed me down on the floor.
Q Did you lose your balance when the baskets pushed you?
A Yes, that is right, sir.
Q And did you look at these baskets when you were sitting there on the floor?
A No, sir. I was looking at my hand.
Q These are the same baskets that you testified to earlier that you saw when you went in the store, is that right?
A That is right.
Q And did you feel any pain?
A I sure did, sir.
Q Where was this pain located?
A In my hand toward my arm was all purple.
Q Is that your right wrist that you are showing us?
A Yes, sir. My whole hand was turned over.
Q What happened then?
A I asked a lady that was there to call my husband and he came in right away and the assistant manager, the manager wasn't there, he said, "Do you want us to get you an ambulance?" My husband said, "No, I want to take my wife to the hospital."
Q Ms. Dominguez, I am going to ask you---Mr. Livingston is standing up again---I am going to ask you to just answer the specific question that I ask and not to anticipate other questions. Okay?
A Okay.

[At this point, Mr. Elder took Ms. Dominguez through a series of questions about the events following the fall. An unknown lady helped the Plaintiff up. An assistant manager (so identified by a badge and white shirt) came up and gave her a box to sit on. Her husband came in and took her by his car to the hospital. They went straight to County Memorial Hospital in downtown London. There, the Plaintiff says, she had to wait "a few hours" because Dr. Ralph Ellman, her doctor, was in the operating room. She had seen Dr. Ellman before, around 1991, for her leg injury, which, the Plaintiff says, was not an injury requiring hospitalization; since that time she has considered Ellman the doctor she "would see for broken bones." The doctor took X-rays, put the arm in a cast, and kept the Plaintiff in the hospital overnight. The next morning he came to see her in the hospital; after that, she went home with her husband. There were several interruptions in this testimony as the witness repeatedly attempted to respond by giving hearsay, making medical conclusions and the like.]

Q Now, were you able to move your fingers with the cast on?
A No, sir.
Q Did the cast completely cover up your fingers?
A Yes, sir, up to my nails.
Q When was the first time you went to see Dr. Ellman after you were released from the hospital?
A The first time?

Q   Yes, ma'am.
A   A week later on.
Q   Did Dr. Ellman do anything at this time?
A   Every time I went he would have an X-ray made of my hand with the cast on.
Q   Did he ever trim any part of the cast off?
A   No, not until about a month later.
Q   Then what happened?
A   He took the cast off and my whole hand was swollen.
Q   He took the cast off about a month later, is that right?
A   That is right.
Q   Did you have any more discomfort?
A   Oh, yes. My hand was painful and so swollen. I could not lift my hand up or nothing. It was dead.
Q   Did it ever swell up?
A   Yes, sir. It was real swollen.
Q   Was it discolored as if it were bruised?
A   Yes, sir.
Q   As a result of this did Dr. Ellman do anything?
A   No, he told me----
Q   (Interrupting.) I am not asking you that. Can you answer the question that I asked you?
A   Well, he told to try two days at home.
Q   Ms. Dominguez, it is not admissible for you to say what the doctor told you and I am asking you what was done, what the doctor did. Now, did the doctor ever do anything after you had this discomfort with your hand after the cast was removed?
A   No.
Q   Did you continue to go back to his office?
A   I went the next day. He told me to go the next day.
Q   Did any other doctor see you?
A   Yes, sir. When I was in the hospital, Dr. Bowers.
Q   But you did go back to the hospital after this, is that right?
A   Yes, sir.
Q   How long was it after the cast was taken off before you went back into the hospital?
A   Three days.
Q   So you were back in the hospital. What hospital was this?
A   County Memorial. The same one in town.
Q   How long did you stay at the hospital this time?
A   Two weeks.
Q   Two weeks. Before you left the hospital again was another cast put on your arm?
A   No. They did not put me in a cast. They just gave me treatment.
Q   What did the treatment consist of?
A   It was an awful painful thing. I will never forget it.
Q   What did they do?
A   They would pull my fingers and put my arm in a whirlpool of water real fast and the water would hit my arm real hard and then some of the nurses would pull my fingers to get my bones straight.
Q   How long did these treatments continue?
A   Two weeks.
Q   Afterwards was there any treatment that you had to do at home or bathing that you had to do at home?
A   I had to bathe my arm in salt water.
Q   After this accident, Ms. Dominguez, was there anything that you were unable to do that you were able to do before the accident?

A Yes, sir. I cannot sweep the floors or mop the floors.
Q Who would help you do this work?
A My husband at nights.
Q Did you have friends who would help you?
A Once in awhile one would come to help.
Q Did Mrs. Pauline Martinez ever help you?
A She gave me a lot of help that woman.
Q How long was it before you were able to use your right arm after the accident?
A About a year and a half.
Q Is this before you could do anything with it or before you could use it to sweep and mop?
A Well, up to this day I cannot hardly do what I used to really do before.
Q It is no longer swollen?
A No, sir.
Q And it is no longer bruised?
A No, sir.
Q You are not telling the jury, are you, that your hand is just like you had to wear a sling, are you?
A No, sir.
Q So approximately how long was it before you became able to lift some small light things with it?
A It was about two years and a half later.
Q Two years and a half?
A Yes.
Q Before you could lift anything?
A Well, I tried to lift sometimes but I just could not do it.
Q Are you able to do shopping now?
A Yes, sir.
Q Are you able to do your housecleaning now?
A Yes, sir.
Q And are you able to do the other work that you need to do, is that right?
A That is right.
Q You are testifying that you do have some disability?
A I do. That is right.
Q How long was it after this accident that you continued to have pain in your wrist?
A That pain don't go away at all. Sometimes it still hurts.

    MR. ELDER: Pass the witness.

CROSS EXAMINATION (EXCERPT FROM TRANSCRIPT)

BY MR. LIVINGSTON:
Q Ms. Dominguez, if I could trouble you for just a moment to come over to the blackboard, and I do not know if your artist skills are any better than my artist skills---
A (Interrupting.) I am not good at that.
Q Will you draw as best you can a diagram of where the bascarts were located in relation to where you came into the store?
A Sir, I cannot draw nothing. I don't know how to draw in the first place.
Q You cannot draw?
A No, sir. I know what you mean but I can't draw.
Q You cannot draw? All right. Please have your seat. Now, you have told this jury that you made an inspection of the baskets, is that right?
A No. I just grabbed one.
Q You did not look at the baskets at all?

A No.
Q You did not glance at them?
A No.
Q So you do not know anything about the baskets, you just walked up and started to pull on the basket?
A Yes, but there were quite a few baskets together that were stuck when I tried to get me one of the baskets.

   * * *

Q Did you just pull like this or did you just really pull?
A I pulled light but they were all stuck together.
Q All of these baskets came rolling right into you when you pulled with your right hand?
A That is right.
Q You are sure that you pulled with your right hand?
A I pulled with my right hand.
Q Have you ever had a basket stick inside before?
A A lot of times. A lot of times.
Q So you knew that this could happen?
A Yes, but I did not know the whole thing would come toward me.
Q Well, why did you pull so hard?
A I had to pull it so I could get one.
Q Did you pull on it and then jerk it again?
A No, the whole thing came toward me.

   * * *

Q And you fell and you broke your right hand?
A That is right.
Q But you pulled the baskets out with your right hand?
A I did. I do everything with my right hand. I am not a left person.
Q And yet when you fell you landed on your right hand?
A Yes. That is right.
Q All right. Now, did Mrs. Martinez come over to see you from time to time?
A She did. She came nearly every other day to see how I was getting along.
Q How long have you all been close friends?
A Twenty-six years as long as I have been in London.
Q Do you know how many rows of carts there were right behind that check-out counter?
A No.
Q Actually when you walked in through the turnstile you were just right at the carts so you did not have a chance to even look at them and look to see how many rows of carts there were, did you?
A No, sir.
Q It was that quick and you just walked up and pulled on one?
A That is right.
Q What did you do differently this time that you hadn't done on other occasions when the carts would stick when you pulled them?
A I don't remember.
Q Well, do you remember, Ms. Dominguez, when your deposition was taken and I asked you whether you had ever had one stick like that? Do you remember that?
A No, sir. I do not remember.
Q It is your testimony though today that you had had them stick on many occasions, is that correct?
A That is right.
Q This is just something that carts do is stick, isn't that right?
A Yes, sir.

MR. LIVINGSTON: Pass the witness.

REDIRECT EXAMINATION (EXCERPT FROM TRANSCRIPT)

BY MR. ELDER:

Q Ms. Dominguez, for the sake of clarification you are not here to tell the jury you actually bent down and made a close inspection of those baskets are you?

A That is right?

Q But at the same time you are not here to try to leave the impression with the jury that you just walked in there and reached around without even looking are you?

A No, sir.

Q You did look at those carts before you took a cart?

MR. LIVINGSTON: Your Honor, we object to Counsel leading the witness and it is repetitious.

THE COURT: Sustained.

MR. ELDER: Judge, the reason I was asking that questions was because it was asked two different ways.

THE COURT: Approach the bench.

(Conference at the bench.)

Q Ms. Dominguez, it is apparent there are responses to the question two different ways. I understood you to answer me when you answered one way and when you answered Mr. Livingston another way.

MR. LIVINGSTON: Excuse me. Your Honor, we object to Counsel testifying.

THE COURT: Sustained.

Q Did you look at the baskets?

MR. LIVINGSTON: We object to this as being repetitious, Your Honor.

THE COURT: Overruled.

Q Did you look at those baskets?

A I looked at them but I did not see how many baskets were there.

Q Did you look at the baskets?

A I looked at them just like that, that is all, when I went to get one.

Q And were you able to form any opinion at that time of those baskets that you saw, the state of repair that those baskets were in that you saw at that time?

MR. LIVINGSTON: Your Honor, we object to Counsel attempting to resurrect his witness and it is repetitious.

THE COURT: Sustained.

* * *

Q Had you any idea, Ms. Dominguez, had you any thought that these baskets as you pull them toward you might knock you off your balance and cause you to fall?

MR. LIVINGSTON: Your Honor, we object to that. It calls for speculation and it is a subjective determination by the witness.

MR. ELDER: I am asking the witness whether she was apprehensive about this, Your Honor.

THE COURT: Sustain the objection.

Q You were not then afraid of being knocked off your balance, were you.

MR. LIVINGSTON: Your Honor, we object to that. That is the same question he just posed to the witness.

THE COURT: Approach the bench.

(Conference at the bench.)

Q After these baskets started rolling towards you, Ms. Dominguez, did you continue to hold on or did you let go of the baskets and reach out to brace yourself?
A I let it go and I lost my balance and I fell on my hand.
Q So you pulled with your right hand?
A Yes, sir.
Q You got knocked off your balance as you reached out, is that your testimony?
A That is right.

MR. ELDER: Pass the witness, Your Honor.

RECROSS EXAMINATION (EXCERPT FROM TRANSCRIPT)

BY MR. LIVINGSTON:
Q Do you remember when we went over to your attorney's office and you took an oath at that time to tell the truth about what happened in this matter?
A That is right, sir.
Q Do you remember being sworn and having a Court Reporter take down your testimony?
A Yes.
Q Do you remember, ma'am when I asked you, and I will read and I want you to read along with me starting at line 11 on page 12:
    QUESTION: Did you ever make any sort of inspection of the baskets?
    ANSWER: No, sir.
That was your testimony at that time, was it not, ma'am?
A Yes, sir.
Q Now, is that your testimony today that you never made any sort of inspection of the baskets?
A I never noticed the baskets when I walked in there.
Q All right. And on this particular day May 7, 1996 you did not make any sort of inspection of the baskets and you didn't make any observation concerning the baskets?
A No, I just went straight on and pulled one. That is all.

MR. LIVINGSTON: Pass the witness, Your Honor.

REDIRECT EXAMINATION (EXCERPT FROM TRANSCRIPT)

BY MR. ELDER:

Q Ms. Dominguez, did you not tell this jury about the condition of the baskets earlier?

   MR. LIVINGSTON: Your Honor, we would object that this is repetitious and it is an attempt of Counsel to resurrect his witness.

   THE COURT: Overruled.

Q Didn't you tell the jury earlier about the condition of the baskets?
A They were old already. Some of them did not have rubber on their wheels when I used to go shopping there. * * *

   MR. LIVINGSTON: Your Honor, we object to Counsel leading the witness.

   THE COURT: Sustained.

Q Did you look at the baskets?
A Yes.

   MR. LIVINGSTON: We object to that as being repetitious.

   THE COURT: Overruled.

Q Ma'am you did look at the baskets?
A Yes, sir.

   MR. LIVINGSTON: Is this on May 7th?

A No, sir. I didn't see the baskets---I didn't notice the baskets how old they were but I know they were pretty old in that store, the baskets.

   MR. LIVINGSTON: Your Honor, we object to the answer given and the question posed as not pertaining to May 7, 1996.

   THE COURT: Let's proceed on questions and answers.

Q And these baskets, Ms. Dominguez, that you are talking about are they the baskets that were there that you are now testifying that are the baskets that were there when you fell down?

   MR. LIVINGSTON: Your Honor, we object to that. It calls for sheer speculation and surmise on the part of this witness.

   THE COURT: Sustained.

Q It is your testimony that the baskets that caused you to lose your balance were stuck together and were in bad repair?
A That is right.

   MR. LIVINGSTON: We object to that as being repetitious and is an attempt by Counsel by leading questions to bolster the testimony of his witness.

   THE COURT: Sustained.

   MR. ELDER: I have no further questions.

MR. LIVINGSTON: I have no questions, Your Honor.

THE COURT: You may step down.

MR. ELDER: I call Mrs. Martinez.

MRS. JOE E. MARTINEZ
first having been duly sworn, in response to questions propounded to her,
testified as follows:

DIRECT EXAMINATION (EXCERPT FROM TRANSCRIPT)

BY MR. ELDER:

[In response to Mr. Elder's questions, Ms. Martinez states her name and gives her age as 49. She says she
has known Ms. Dominguez 20 years. Before the injury, she testifies, the two women were neighbors and
she used to visit Ms. Dominguez. Ms. Dominguez's health was "okay," according to the witness; she was
able to do all her work without help. The witness testifies to having shopped at this Scott's store for 20
years and states that she observed the equipment in the store.]

Q Did you ever have occasion to observe the shopping baskets there?

MR. LIVINGSTON: Your Honor, we object to the questions as being irrelevant
and immaterial and not put into any time frame.

THE COURT: Overruled.

Q Immediately prior to the accident that Ms. Dominguez sustained, did you have
   any observation of the shopping baskets in the store?
A Well, I had the same trouble that she did.
Q Did you observe the baskets immediately prior?
A They did need fixing up.
Q I beg your pardon.
A They needed fixing up. They were kind of bad.

MR. LIVINGSTON: Your Honor, we object to this. The baskets are not identified in any manner as being the baskets that are involved in this matter. The
previous witness has testified that there were approximately fifty baskets in the
store. We object to the question as calling for sheer speculation.

THE COURT: Overruled.

Q Mrs. Martinez, after Ms. Dominguez got out of the hospital did you help her
   with any of her housework?
A No, I didn't.
Q Okay. But you did visit her. Did you have occasion to see her and be with
   her?
A Yes, I did.
Q Did she ever complain of any pain or difficulty?
A Yes, she did.
Q What sort of complaints did she have?
A Well, she didn't---she couldn't move her hand too good because it was in the
   cast with just her fingers sticking out.
Q I see. And after she got the cast off did she have any difficulty that you
   could see.

A Yes, she did.
Q What sort of difficulty did she have after she got the cast off?
A Well, some things she could not pick up, you know, it would be weak and she couldn't do too much. * * *

MR. ELDER: Pass the witness.

CROSS EXAMINATION (EXCERPT FROM TRANSCRIPT)

BY MR. LIVINGSTON:
Q Mrs. Martinez, is it your testimony that you never saw any new baskets in that store?
A New baskets? Well, they have had baskets all the time but I was not seeing if they were new or not. I just got a basket.
Q You just went and got a basket and you used the basket?
A Yes.
Q You don't know anything about Scott's method of repairing these baskets and renewing the condition of these baskets, do you, ma'am?
A No, I do not.

MR. LIVINGSTON: Pass the witness, Your Honor.

MR. ELDER: No futher questions.

THE COURT: You are excused.

MR. ELDER: The Plaintiff rests.

THE COURT: The jury will stand recessed for a ten-minute coffee break.

D. DEFENDANT'S MOTION FOR JUDGMENT AS MATTER OF LAW

TRANSCRIPT OF THE PROCEEDINGS

MR. LIVINGSTON: The Defendant's Motion.

Comes now the Defendant, Scott's Food Store, at the close of Plaintiff's case, and respectfully moves this Honorable Court to withdraw this case from the jury and return a judgment on the undisputed evidence in favor of Defendant and against Plaintiff for all the relief sought and prayed for herein for each and all of the following reasons:
1. No evidence of any probative value has been adduced upon which the jury might find that any singular condition of the carts in general or any defect in the carts caused the occurrence in question; the proof as adduced showing solely that the carts were stuck together and at the time that Ms. Dominguez pulled on them, four carts came out at once rather than the one that she expected.
2. Although there is some testimony in the record that on the occasion in question the carts may or may not have been rusted and in ill repair, there is no testimony in this record that such ill repair or rust in any manner caused or contributed to the accident in question. Therefore there is no evidence upon which the jury could predicate a finding that this Defendant knew or should have known of any condition of the carts occasioning the accident to Ms. Dominguez in view of the fact that there is no evidence as to what caused the condition in question; and further any supposition by the jury as to proximate cause would be pure speculation in that there is no showing that any condition, i.e., rust or

ill repair of the carts in any manner contributed to cause or did cause the occurrence in question.

WHEREFORE premises considered the Defendant prays that the Court withdraw this case from the jury and return a judgment on the undisputed evidence in favor of this Defendant and against this Plaintiff for all relief sought and prayed for herein.

                    Respectfully submitted,

                    McIntosh and Walker

                    By: Robert L. Livingston, Jr.
                    Attorneys for the Defendant.

    THE COURT: The motion is overruled.

E. NOTES AND QUESTIONS ON THE TRIAL

1. EVIDENCE. Notice how important the rules of evidence are to a trial attorney. Although evidence principles are largely beyond the probable scope of your course, the examinations thus far have exposed you to the following principles: (a) The hearsay rule of exclusion; (b) hearsay exceptions; (c) the requirements of personal knowledge unless the witness is an expert; (d) relevance; (e) the form of examination (including the preference for non-leading questions on direct examination); (f) impeachment by use of prior inconsistent statement.

2. DISCRETION IN EVIDENCE RULINGS. The rules of evidence often allow the judge considerable discretion. Here, for example, a major evidence controversy has concerned the admissibility of testimony regarding baskets other than those that injured plaintiff, on days other than the incident in question. Notice how the judge ruled: he initially excluded this evidence, but then apparently changed his mind and admitted it.

3. OBJECTIONS. The party with the burden of proof is typically attempting to introduce evidence; the opposing party ordinarily uses the rules of evidence to exclude as much evidence as possible. Note how the defendant's attorney has exploited the rules to limit the plaintiff's proof. Rules regarding hearsay, personal knowledge and leading questions can sometimes significantly hamper the examination of unsophisticated witnesses.

4. METHOD AND SEQUENCE OF DIRECT EXAMINATION. In spite of the popular emphasis upon cross examination, many observers believe that direct examination is more important and more difficult. Notice Plaintiff's attorney's skill at controlling the examination and rephrasing questions so that evidence is received and understood.

Skillful direct examination is an art, but it frequently involves the following elements: (a) identification of the witness and placement of that witness in context; (b) clear designation by date and time of the event in question; (c) questions that produce the story in chronological order; (d) use of simple terminology and graphic details; (e) re-orientation of the jury when the subject of examination shifts or when technical questions, such as evidentiary predicates, are at issue.

5. MOTION FOR JUDGMENT AS A MATTER OF LAW. Plaintiff's evidence is largely circumstantial, with the only direct evidence being that of plaintiff—to the extent that it is believed plaintiff observed the baskets. What is the standard for a judgment as a matter of law—and should the motion be granted here, or is plaintiff's evidence sufficient to present a jury issue?

6. **DEFENDANT'S EVIDENCE.** Defendant is not required to present evidence under these circumstances, but it did so. In the actual case, Defendant's evidence (which appears on the following pages) was not helpful to Defendant. It inadvertently strengthened Plaintiff's case. Even careful preparation is often insufficient to avoid that result.

F. THE TRIAL: DEFENDANT'S EVIDENCE

TRANSCRIPT OF THE PROCEEDINGS

GEORGE FRANKLIN
first having been duly sworn, in response to questions propounded to him, testified as follows:

DIRECT EXAMINATION (EXCERPT FROM TRANSCRIPT)

BY MR. LIVINGSTON:

Q State your name, please, sir.

A My name is George Franklin.

Q For whom are you employed?

A Scott's Food Store.

Q And what is your position of employment?

A I am a property accountant.

Q What is a property accountant?

A I keep records of all the equipment that is purchased for Scott's.

Q During a given year are a number of carts purchased for the Scott's chain?

A Yes, there are.

Q Have you researched your records to ascertain when prior to May, 1996 your records reflect that new carts were specifically assigned to Store No. 14?

A Yes, I have.

Q If you would, sir, refer to those records, and am I correct in assuming that you as property accountant would be in charge of preparing those records?

A Yes, I am.

Q If you will review those records and tell to the jury, Mr. Franklin when prior to May of 1996 were new carts last ordered by the Scott's chain for Store No. 14 and specifically delivered?

A In our fifth period of '94-'95 which would be between October 22nd and November 18, 1994 we sent to Store No. 14 fifty carts.

Q Would those be new carts?

A Those would be brand-new carts.

Q Let me ask you something about how Scott's operates from the standpoint of these carts. Once fifty carts would be assigned to No. 14 and some of thoses carts would be lost from whose stock would they be normally replenished?

A We have in our shop a large amount of carts which are constantly being repaired and as stores need carts we send from this shop the repaired carts.

Q So the entire number of new carts purchased during any given one year may or may not end up at any particular store, is that correct?

A That is correct.

Q How many in number and amount of new carts were purchased for Scott's during the year 1994?

A In that fiscal year, '94-'95, which is one year, we purchased $123,911 worth of carts.

Q Do you know the number?

A No, I don't. They would be in the neighborhood of $30 per cart.

MR. LIVINGSTON: Pass the witness.

CROSS EXAMINATION (EXCERPT FROM TRANSCRIPT)

BY MR. ELDER:

[Mr. Elder begins cross examination by establishing that at $30 per cart, $123,911 would purchase something in excess of 4100 carts. Upon being asked the number of Scott's stores, the witness is not sure but "I would say around ninety." Mr. Elder establishes that the witness does not actually supervise delivery of the carts to the store; he is told that they are shipped and keeps records. "So you are not giving any direct evidence that they might have gotten there, they may have gone to store 15?" Mr. Elder asks. "It is possible," the witness answers.]

Q And I believe that you have testified that you have a shop where they are being constantly repaired. Can you tell the jury why they are being repaired?

A Well, your casters a lot of time might stick and be hard to push, or maybe a car may run into them and they may get bent up that way, or they don't roll easy so they are picked up by a truck and delivered to the shop to be repaired so that they will be easy to push in the store.

Q And similarly to avoid having a bunch of them stick together when you try to pull one loose to avoid having a whole bunch of them coming. Would this be a fair statement within your knowledge?

A Within my knowledge.

Q I would assume that it is of your knowledge that if these carts are not in a good state of repair, they can be and are likely to be dangerous to the customers of Scott's, is that correct?

A That is correct.

Q And Scott's realizes this danger and that is why they have a repair facility, is that correct?

A That is correct.

MR. ELDER: I have no further questions of this witness.

MR. LIVINGSTON: No questions.

THE COURT: You are excused.

MR. LIVINGSTON: I call Mr. Douglas.

WAYNE DOUGLAS
first having been duly sworn, in response to questions propounded to him, testified as follows:

DIRECT EXAMINATION (EXCERPT FROM TRANSCRIPT)

BY MR. LIVINGSTON:

[The witness testifies that he lives in Denton, West York, where he works for Scott's Construction as a shop dispatcher and maintenance man. As such, he works on repair of carts and picks up and delivers them. Repairs, he testifies, are necessitated by breakage of casters, cars hitting carts and various other damage. In 1996, he states, the shop maintained a schedule whereby each store was visited for cart repairs every 45 days. In the interim, managers were instructed to call the shop for necessary repairs. Store No. 14, the store at issue here, was a "high loss" store, meaning there was a high rate of cart disappearance.]

Q Approximately how often would you bring baskets to Store No. 14?
A It all depends; sometimes it would be as much as forty-five days and sometimes as much as ninety.
Q And at that time approximately what kind of number of baskets would you bring in?
A Twenty-five to thirty approximately.
Q Now, how many baskets total did this store have inside as a rule?
A Usually from fifty to sixty-five.
Q So if the testimony of Mr. Franklin was that these baskets had been replaced as new in October and November of 1994, according to your testimony, they would have all been replaced again through the process of repair and losing those baskets?
A That is approximately right, sir.
Q Was this store one of the high loss stores of the Scott's chain insofar as these baskets were concerned?
A Yes. It was one of the four stores with the highest loss.

    MR. LIVINGSTON: Pass the witness, Your Honor.

CROSS EXAMINATION (EXCERPT FROM TRANSCRIPT)

Q Mr. Douglas, Mr. Franklin, who testified before you, testified that Scott's has some ninety outlets, is that correct?
A That is right.
Q I assume that you talked with Mr. Livingston before your testimony?
A Sure.
Q Now, you are not here to tell us that any specific quantity of carts was taken to that specific store at or near the month of May, 1996, are you?
A I cannot say so.
Q And you testified that the casters would sometimes go out of these carts. Would other problems happen to them? Would they get rusty?
A Yes, sir, if they stayed out in the weather.
Q And when somebody would leave them out there after they carried the groceries to the car and another car pulls into the parking place, would they not get their frames bent?
A It is possible.
Q All right, sir. And could this not cause a row of them that are stacked nested among each other to stick together so a few of them would stick together?
A It is very, very possible.
Q Now, you said that this store was a high-loss store. Are these areas where a lot of people do not have cars and push grocery carts home?
A Yes, sir.
Q And are very many of these carts recovered in the neighborhoods?
A Most of them are.
Q So this high-loss area that you are talking about it is probably high-loss and probably pretty high recovery of the baskets too, is it not?
A It is a turnover of them.
Q And I would imagine it would be fair to say that sometimes kids would play in the ones that were just setting out on the sidewalks?
A It is possible.
Q And that they get turned over and spend a lot of time lying on their sides?
A Yes, sir.
Q So would it not be fair to say that in these high-loss stores that you have testified about that you would have also probably an extra high incidence of disrepair among the carts, not only just the loss, the ones that are there are

probably not in as good a state of repair as others, would that not be a fair statement?

A Yes, sir.

Q Would this be a fair statement?

A That would be a fair statement.

Q All right. And in spite of this is there any accelerated maintenance for the carts for these stores in the high-loss areas with the high-loss ratio?

A What do you mean by accelerated?

Q Well, do you pay any attention, any greater attention to these particular stores than say you would take to some store out on Fairmont where I assume that everybody drives up in his car and drives off in his car and there is probably not very much bending?

A They get approximately the same, sir.

Q All right. So they don't get any special treatment?

A No.

MR. ELDER: Pass the witness, Your Honor.

REDIRECT EXAMINATION (EXCERPT FROM TRANSCRIPT)

BY MR. LIVINGSTON:

[Mr. Livingston asks how many people work in Scott's Construction on repair of carts. The witness states that there are five trucks, each with one man, "and it is possible that we could have them all going at one time."]

MR. LIVINGSTON: Pass the witness, Your Honor.

MR. ELDER: I have no further questions of this witness, Your Honor.

MR. LIVINGSTON: The Defendant rests.

MR. ELDER: We have no rebuttal.

THE COURT: Both sides rest. Ladies and gentlemen of the jury, you will stand recessed until 9:00 o'clock tomorrow morning. At that time the case will be submitted to you for your deliberation. Good night. Nine o'clock tomorrow morning.

G. RENEWAL OF THE MOTION FOR JUDGMENT AS A MATTER OF LAW

NOTE

At the conclusion of all the evidence, Mr. Livingston renewed his Motion for Judgment as a Matter of Law in substantially the same language. Although aware that the court would likely overrule it, Livingston made the Motion because Fed. R. Civ. P. 50 conditions the right to make a Motion for Judgment as a Matter of Law after trial upon the making of a Motion at the close of all the evidence. Mr. Livingston desired to make a Motion for Judgment as a Matter of Law because it would be more likely to be granted (since it would be made after the trial and would allow for time for research and briefing and for considered reflection by the court.) The court did overrule the renewed Motion.

H. JURY ARGUMENT

EXCERPTS FROM PLAINTIFF'S OPENING ARGUMENT (FROM TRANSCRIPT)

MR. ELDER: Ladies and gentlemen of the jury, I want to thank you for your attention throughout this case. I know it's a sacrifice for many of you to be here, but we appreciate it. And what is more important, you are making the jury system work. There are some countries in the world that do not use juries. There are also people who say that the jury system is inefficient and we should get rid of it. I hope we never come to that. I think we will never see a better system than this one, by depending upon twelve folks who aren't in favor of either side or the other.

Enough of that, though. In a few minutes, the judge will read you a set of instructions and a set of questions called "special interrogatories." A few minutes after that, you will take these questions back with you into the jury room and decide this case. I want to take just a minute to go over these instructions with you, and discuss the questions. What I say to you will come from the evidence that you've heard in the case or from the judge's instruction that I expect the judge will give.

First of all, I expect the judge will define the term "negligence" for you. You remember I talked with you about this definition back during voir dire examination, at the first of the case. "Negligence," the judge will tell you, means "a failure to do that which a person of ordinary prudence, in the exercise of ordinary care, would do under the same or similar circumstances." It's not complicated, it's a very basic and simple concept, and in common-sense terms it means if a person is careless, that's negligence.

Let's stop right there and look at the evidence for a minute. Scott's Food Stores is a grocery store that has all kinds of people come to it. It invites these people by paid advertising--on the radio, TV, in the papers. Having invited all these people in to sell them groceries, Scott's has a duty to use care to protect these invited people from injury of any kind. It sets a standard of safety, and it can set that standard high, with a very safe store, or it can set it low, and say, well, this is a high-loss store in a certain part of town. By your verdict, you'll be saying whether that low standard is right. And remember, this isn't the first time in recorded history that a person has fallen and been injured in a store because of a dangerous condition. It happens all the time, and the evidence showed that it happened to Mrs. Dominguez before. You heard Scott's own witnesses say so. The grocer knows very well that lots of people have been injured in this way and knows about the conditions. The customer doesn't, necessarily.

Remember, the duty to use care depends upon the circumstances of the person. I tell you that the circumstances of Ms. Dominguez are different: she is an elderly lady, 63 years of age, with all the difficulties that elderly ladies have. You saw her; she is a hard-working, honest lady. But she is not as spry as a young store manager. She isn't a brilliant engineer or Ph.D.; she's a housewife. Those people at Scott's repair shop, and the managers, and the overall management of Scott's--well, she has to depend on them to have a safe store.

The judge tells you what "proximate cause" is. Well, it's a simple, common-sense idea too. If the negligence caused this injury, or was a contributing cause to it, if it had anything to do with it, and if it was foreseeable that this was the kind of thing that could happen, or might happen, then that means it's a proximate cause of the injury. What do we have here? You heard the people from Scott's repair shop. With a little prodding, a little questioning from me, they told you this was a foreseeable result of negligence in maintaining the carts. I asked one of them, "A person can injure themself if the carts are defective?" And he said, "That is very, very possible." In fact, that's exactly why they have a repair shop in the first place.

The judge also tells you that the standard you are to use is the preponderance of the evidence. That is also a simple standard. It means the greater weight of credible evidence. So when you look at each of the questions you have here, all you have to do is weigh the evidence on either side and see which side is weightier. You do not have to study the matter until you are absolutely certain about what happened—that's not your job, because it would be impossible—you are to decide each question by the greater weight. Remember the example of the scales. It's which ever way the scales tip, that's the way you answer the question.

Now, let's get down to the questions themselves. The questions are called special issues. Let's look at special issue number one.

Special issue number one asks, "Do you find from the preponderence of the evidence that the carts supplied on the occasion in question by Defendant, its agents or employees were bent and defective?" Let's look at the evidence here. I wish Scott's had called in some of their employees who worked at the store there, these employees are under Scott's control and they could get them here easily, but they haven't because their testimony wouldn't help Scott's at all. I think you can infer from that alone what the condition of the baskets were. Miranda Dominguez tells you what the condition of the baskets was; they were old, they were rusty. Mr. Dominguez tells you: people would take them out, leave them in the rain, cars would run into them, kids would play with them and bang them together. Ms. Martinez was in the store immediately before this accident. She tells you the carts were bent and defective. Thelma Rodriguez was in the store. She tells you the same thing. Then, the gentlemen from Scott's repair shop—they tell you, I think quite honestly, about the condition of the baskets. The baskets had been put in that store about two years before. This was a high-loss store. People would take the baskets out of this store and take them away and damage them more than at almost any other store. Yet they had no extra degree of repairs from this store. They knew that baskets from these stores became bent and defective faster than at other stores. They tell you what can happen: People get injured, among other things.

Also, you can consider the evidence about the accident itself—how it happened. An elderly lady pulls on a cart. She is not an extra-strong person, in fact she can't pull as hard as most of us. Yet the carts came out, four or five stuck together, and run her over. Why? Because the carts were stuck together. That happens from them being bent and defective.

I think when you consider all the evidence, including that from the defendant's own witnesses, you almost have to come to the conclusion that the answer to special issue number one has to be that you do find the baskets to have been bent and defective, by the greater weight of the evidence. So I think you have to say "we do."

Now, let's look at special issue number 2. That question asks you a very simple thing: "Do you find from a preponderance of the evidence that such conduct, if any you have found, was negligent, as that term has been defined?" in its failure to repair or replace the carts inquired about in special issue number 2. Here, the jury sets the standard. The jury says whether or not we should have safe stores. And the way the jury does that, is by either saying that this dangerous condition was all right, or by saying that the utter failure to repair or replace these baskets in a reasonable way was careless, which I think unquestionably it was.

Remember what negligence means. It's the failure to do that which an ordinarily prudent person would do under the circumstances. In other words, there is a standard. Anything less than the standard is negligence. Of course, a person can be very careful, fairly careful, sort of careful, ordinarily careful, careless, or very careless. Scott's says they were trying to run a high-loss store. They were trying not to be more careful than they absolutely had to be. In that situation, they are endangering people--not just profits. Look at the standard. If they did anything less than the standard, then they were negligent.

They got these carts new about two years before. They left them out in the rain. They left them out for kids to play with. They knew it was a high-loss area, and that meant they would have a higher incidence of damage to baskets. They also knew that this higher incidence of damage to baskets would mean a higher incidence of damage to people. Yet they had no special program to take care of this. Were they careful? Were they prudent? Is this what an ordinarily prudent person would have done if running a grocery store? More importantly, is it the kind of standard we want to set here, in a court of law, as the kind of maintenance we want for grocery stores that the entire public, from young children to elderly people to handicapped people, are going to use? I would state to you that there is no question that it simply was not prudent under the circumstances, and I think the answer to the question almost has to be "yes," we do find that this failure to repair or replace the carts was negligence.

The next issue, number 3, asks you whether the negligence was a proximate cause of the occurrence in question. Remember the testimony of their own witnesses: That's the reason they have a repair shop in the first place, is simply that defective, bent, rusty carts cause injuries. I believe from the evidence that you should answer "yes," or in other words "we do," to this question.

Now in special issue number 4, the question asks you whether you find that Mrs. Dominguez failed to keep such a lookout for her safety as would a person in the exercise of ordinary care. First of all, in this question the burden of proof is on Scott's stores to prove by a preponderance of the evidence that Ms. Dominguez was herself to blame in this accident. Scott's has attempted to shift the blame away from their own failure to repair or replace the baskets, to shift that blame onto Miranda Dominguez. Well, I don't think there's any evidence and certainly not a preponderance of the evidence that says Scott's ought to be able to shift the blame onto her this way. You saw Ms. Dominguez testify. She is not nearly as learned in the law as Mr. Livingston. He went to a fine law school. She has a high school education. He tried to trip her up, and several times he did trip her up. But I tell you one thing: I think it's clear from the way she testified that she told you the truth, and in fact I think it's clear from her testimony that she couldn't lie if she had to. What did her testimony establish? She did not expect to fall. Does she have a duty to meticulously inspect the baskets before she takes one, or can she hope that the store has done its job? How many of you make a meticulous inspection of grocery carts when you walk in the store? Nobody. And she tells you how she pulled on the baskets; she pulled lightly, the baskets were stuck, she pulled slightly harder--she had to, because the basket wouldn't come out--and then five or six baskets, totally unexpectedly, came out at her and knocked her down. She is an elderly lady. She was not a teenager barging in. Scott's should keep its baskets in good enough shape so that elderly customers don't have to go over them with a magnifying glass before assuming they're safe. For that reason, I think the answer to this special issue ought to be "no," we do not find that Scott's has proved to us that the blame should be placed on Ms. Dominguez.

Special issue number 5 does not have to be answered if you answer "we do not" to special issue number 4. Therefore, I don't think you should answer special issue number 5 at all.

[In similar fashion, plaintiff's attorney argued that the answer to special issue number 6 should be "we do not," and that special issue number 7 should not be answered. He also argued that even if the proximate causation issue were to be answered (issue 7), the answer would have to be "we do not" because Ms. Dominguez could not have anticipated what would happen to her.]

Special issue number 8 asks about damages. Remember what I asked all of you at the beginning of this case: If you find that there has been substantial pain and suffering, and pain and suffering includes discomfort, pain, disability, the degree to which your life is lessened by having a wrist that permanently is set so that it is at a bent angle from your arm—if you find that all of this is substantial, could you award substantial damages? You all told me you could. Look at the lady. Who would want to have an arm and wrist like she has? I tell you frankly, there is simply not any way that any amount of money can compensate for the taking away of the ability to fully use a wrist or arm. But all that the law can do is attempt to do it. That is what you ladies and gentlemen are here for.

The first part of the question asks you, What damage has she had for pain and mental anguish in the past? There are three ways you can figure this question. First, you could say there is none—because pain and mental anguish is something you can't see. Well, if you did that, it would be a violation of your oaths, and so that possibility is out. Second, you can guess at a figure. But that would be a violation of your oaths too, because your verdict is supposed to be based on the evidence. So the third way, I think, is the right way. You can figure she was 17 months under the care of the doctor, and that is when pain, suffering and mental discomfort is greatest. She couldn't even take care of her bodily functions alone then. 17 months is 510 days of discomfort and dependence on others for everything. What is that worth to a person, to avoid that? I would say that ten dollars a day, to avoid the period of most intense discomfort and utter dependence upon others, is absolutely minimal. I am talking about a day that is, minute by minute, hour by hour, continuous discomfort and the knowledge that you can't do housework, you are an utterly nonproductive human being, you have to have others drive you to the doctor, sweep the floor, feed you, even aid you in bodily functions, do all the things for you that made you a productive human being. This minimal figure of ten dollars per day, over the span of 510 days lived minute by minute, would be fifty-one hundred dollars, just by itself.

And that is not all. It has been five years since the incident. Ms. Dominguez still cannot lift heavy things. She will never be able to. For 2 1/2 years, she could not lift anything at all. She still has discomfort, still has the mental knowledge that her arm is deformed. Five years later, you can clearly see the difference in her two arms. Now, the period of most intense suffering is past, but I tell you that for the rest of her life she will carry with her the badge of this occurrence in May of 1996. Figure it at less per day, there still are many thousands of dollars that cannot help but be added. The court specifically tells you to compute future pain and mental anguish. I have put down a total figure in the petition: $ 75,000. I thought the evidence would support that figure and I still do. However, I have to set an upper limit for you, and that's all I was trying to do by the $ 75,000 figure. We've brought you the evidence. You give the answer.

In summary, then, I think we've shown you that Scott's was at fault. We've brought you the evidence to do that by a preponderance of the evidence. Scott's wants to shift the blame onto Ms. Dominguez. I don't think they have shown you by a preponderance of the evidence that she was. I think the evidence shows that she was substantially injured. I have simply argued that you should follow this evidence and render a verdict accordingly, and that is what I urge you to do.

EXCERPTS FROM DEFENDANT'S JURY ARGUMENT (FROM TRANSCRIPT)

MR. LIVINGSTON: Ladies and gentlemen of the jury, I too want to thank you for taking time from your usual business to come here and serve as jurors. This system--the jury system--is the best that has ever been devised for deciding disputes or lawsuits. You are part of a long history through which this system has evolved and been perfected.

You will notice that one of the first things that the judge tells you is "Do not let bias, prejudice or sympathy play any part in your deliberations." It is easy to look at the plaintiff and say, "I will find in her favor because I have sympathy for her." It is easy to look at a company and say to yourself, unconsciously, "Well, maybe it's not all that bad to hold against the company even though nothing has really been shown to indicate it was at fault." But that would be wrong.

The judge's instructions will tell you that you are the sole judges of the credibility of the witnesses and the weight to be given their testimony. You can believe or disbelieve all or any part of any witness' testimony. How do you make the decision? By seeing whether they have a bias in their testimony, such as desire for recovery from a company or friendship of long standing for some other witness. By seeing how they testify--whether it is contradictory, whether it is consistent.

Notice that the judge will tell you, as Mr. Elder has said, that everything must be proven by the preponderance of the evidence. We require this of every person who comes into court making claims against someone else. You cannot speculate, you cannot guess, you must follow the evidence. That means two things-- first of all, there must be evidence on every issue you decide--and not just speculation; and second, the evidence must be stronger and more convincing than the contrary evidence.

Let's look at the special interrogatories you must answer. First of all, special interrogatory number one asks you whether you find from a preponderance of the evidence that the carts pulled by the Plaintiff on the occasion in question were bent and defective. Let's stop there a minute. What evidence is there that those four or five baskets that came out at the plaintiff, according to her testimony, were "bent?" None. No witness said they were. What is the credibility of the witnesses on this point? Remember you are the judges of the credibility of the witnesses. There simply are none. The incident occurred on May 7, 1996. They didn't bring suit until late in 1998, nearly two years later. Just think about that, if you will. Here is the plaintiff, alleging that Scott's was so negligent, and she was so severely injured, yet she waits nearly two years to sue. By that time, you see, it is very hard for Scott's to tell you what happened out there that day or the exact condition of the exact cart that she pulled on. And what is the testimony of Ms. Dominguez? Well, on direct examination by her attorney she said she didn't observe the carts. On the deposition I read to her, here in court, her deposition taken after this suit was filed by her attorney, she said she never made any inspection of those carts. When I cross-examined here she said again that she never even looked at the carts. Now, all this, after she has waited about two years before suing, so that we can't pin-point the carts in question. What can we do? We did what we could to show you. All we can do is show you what we do. Scott's operates a full-time, full-staffed repair shop to keep these baskets in good condition. When a cart is damaged too severely to repair, we replace it. I want to point out one thing that has been said by plaintiff's attorney that could be misleading. He said the carts were put in new two years ago. While that's true, the evidence is very clear that we were constantly replacing carts, constantly turning them over, so that there were constantly new carts coming into the store.

There simply is no evidence that the carts in question were bent or defective. We don't even know why they stuck together, if they did. It could have been a popsickle stick put there by a child, that wedged in between carts, for all we know. It could have been the last customer, who pushed the carts in too hard. But as Ms. Dominguez herself admitted, "Sticking is just something that carts do." When you nest a cart, and you have to nest them to get them all into the store, you have to assume some sticking even if the carts are in perfect condition. Because of that, should Scott's become liable to pay 25,000 dollars? No. The answer to special interrogatory number one, based on the evidence, has to be "we do not."

Special interrogatory number two asks you whether Scott's was guilty of negligence. I want to point out that there is no evidence about these carts. They may have been brought in that very day, for all plaintiff knows. All we have been able to show is that we did repair and replace them, systematically. So I think the evidence about the first part of the question is pretty clearcut.

What is negligence? A person is negligent if he or she fails to use ordinary care. It's as simple as that. What is ordinary care for a grocer? What would an ordinary grocer do in this instance? Get rid of all his carts, because they sometimes stick, and the sticking is unavoidable? Of course not. I suggest to you that an ordinary grocer would do just what Scott's did here: use bascarts, because they are the best known type of carts; and have a facility for repair so you can be sure the wheels are running, etc. In fact, Scott's had a full-time repair shop, with full-time people and five trucks running constantly to keep these bascarts not only safe, but easily running and attractive for the public.

Remember, although this is a company, it's madeup of individuals. There is a store manager and assistant manager. They are human beings. They are not supermen. They do not have X-ray vision or any superpowers. They cannot prevent all accidents. Please do not expect them to be supermen. Please follow the law. The law says they have to exercise "ordinary care"--the degree of care that an ordinary person in the position of a grocer would exercise. I believe they have exercised a great deal more than that. I think from the evidence your answer to special interrogatory two has to be "we do not" find Scott's and its employees guilty. There is no evidence to find them guilty of negligence.

[Defendant's attorney argued against an affirmative finding on proximate causation (issue 3), then argued for an affirmative finding on issue 4 and 6 (contributory negligence) and issues 5 and 7 (proximate causation on contributory negligence).]

Finally, special issue number eight asks you how much money, if paid now in cash, should Scott's pay to Ms. Dominguez. I want to point out a couple of things. First of all, she shows you no medical bills, does not put those costs into evidence, and the judge does not instruct you to find any. Those are out of the case. If they were sigificant and if they were really related to the case, you can bet plaintiff's attorney would have asked for them and put them into evidence. But there aren't any, and you know the reason, and you can't consider or guess or speculate about them. Secondly, the doctor is not here at all. I disagree with Mr. Elder about the reason the doctor was not called. They could use the doctor to show the actual painfulness if any and the actual disaability if any. Future physical pain and mental anguish? There might be evidence if the doctor was here. But there isn't any, and that's why the doctor isn't here, or one reason why he isn't here. There isn't any evidence, unless you want to guess or speculate. Let's look at what you saw. You watched her manipulate her arm. There is full movement, no swelling, no difference unless you look very closely, to tell one wrist from the other. There are no records past March of 1997, no medical records at all, no medical evidence at all past that date. And that's a year, or nearly a year, before this suit was even brought. Everything indicates a full recovery. Otherwise, there would be medical testimony from plaintiff's own doctor, the doctor she chose to treat her. And I might add, it's simply not true that the doctor would have to be here and wait around and that it would cost a lot of money to bring him. His deposition can be taken in his own office at a time convenient to him, and at nominal cost, and that deposition could be brought to you ladies and gentlemen. That wasn't done, because it would not have been helpful to the plaintiff.

And I want to point out one more thing. Counsel for Ms. Dominguez has tried to get you to multiply a certain figure times each day in order to compare what he calls "minimal" damages that Scott's should pay to Ms. Dominguez. I don't think the damages he computed are "minimal," and I think it's subject to manipulation of figures and gives misleading results. I ask you to look at the question whether the damage computed is reasonable as a whole. I think $ 75,000 dollars for a broken wrist completely healed, is ridiculous, and I think you know it is; it's exaggerated, like many other things in this suit. I think if you look at the overall reasonableness of the figure at issue here; you'd have to put down maybe $ 1,000--that's at the most. I ask you to answer each of the questions according to the evidence, without bias or prejudice or sympathy. Thank you.

EXCERPTS FROM PLAINTIFF'S CLOSING ARGUMENT (FROM TRANSCRIPT)

MR. ELDER: I want to take a minute to respond to some of the things that have been said by defense counsel. I have no quarrel with Mr. Livingston personally, of course; he's just representing his client, but I think you have to remember that that's what he is doing. Defense counsel tells you that there's no evidence about the condition of the carts. He tells you I can't isolate the specific cart that was in issue here. That's true. He tells you that Ms. Dominguez did not make a minute inspection of the cart. And that's true too: she looked at it like a shopper getting a basket to go shopping, and after the injury I'm sure she was more concerned about going to the hospital than in trying to make a minute inspection of the cart so she could answer all of the questions here in minute detail. But I also think that Mr. Livingston is ignoring the evidence. Mr. Dominguez said he saw the bascarts on this very occasion. They were rusty and bent. Ms. Dominguez tells you that although she did not bend down to make a close inspection, and you know no shopper does that, honestly, she did see that they were in bad condition. Mrs. Martinez and Mrs. Rodriguez tell you the same thing. And although Mr. Dominguez doesn't tell you this, you are entitled to make common sense conclusions from the evidence. You don't leave your common sense behind you when you go into the jury box. Well, why do five or six carts stick together? And I tell you, it isn't because a kid has left a popsicle stick.

And you are entitled to consider the testimony of Scott's own witnesses. They say that this was a high-loss store, with particular problems about the carts getting into a dangerous condition. But they did not do anything to correct for that. Mr. Livingston tells you that this is what an ordinary, prudent grocer would do. I disagree. You are setting the standard. The simple fact is that they knew these carts were dangerous, but they follow this kind of procedure in their high-loss stores. If the lady had been shopping at a store in the Fairmont area, or in some other wealthy area, she would not have had to face this kind of dangerous condition.

Mr. Livingston tells you that Mrs. Dominguez must have been negligent. Now, on that issue, it's up to Scott's to prove she was negligent. Compare the evidence of Scott's negligence, the proof we have made, with their claim that they have proved it was her fault. I tell you they have not shown any such thing. I think it's disgraceful, in an attempt to shift the blame off them, to try to say that she must have been negligent because otherwise she would not have been injured. For one thing, remember that the standard for negligence depends upon the circumstances. An elderly lady going into a store is simply not in the same position as the grocer to prevent an accident.

Finally, Mr. Livingston ridicules the notion that Ms. Dominquez's damage is substantial. I ask you whether anyone would want to be in her place. She had a horribly injured wrist, with the bone literally stiking out, and she had to wait for a doctor. The pain lasted month after month. The wrist swelled so that she had to return to the hospital. It is deformed and will be for the rest of her life. I ask for a just verdict, based on evidence, that Scott's was negligent, that Mrs. Dominguez was not, and that she suffered at least $ 75,000 in damages. Thank you.

I. CHARGE AND VERDICT

NOTE ON PREPARATION OF THE CHARGE

Prior to jury argument, the attorneys submitted requested written charges. The judge adopted the special interrogatories proposed by each respective party, but used standard form definitions and instructions. Fed. R. Civ. P. 51 requires the judge to inform the attorneys of his action on their requested charges. In this case, the judge furnished them with a written charge before argument began.

CHARGE OF THE COURT CONTAINING
JURY'S ANSWERS TO SPECIAL INTERROGATORIES

MEMBERS OF THE JURY: This case is submitted to you on special interrogatories consisting of specific questions about the facts, which you must decide from the evidence you have heard in this trial. You are the sole judges of the credibility of the witnesses and the weight to be given their testimony, but in matters of law, you must be governed by the instructions in this charge. In discharging your responsibility on this jury, you will observe all the instructions which have previously been given you. I shall now give you additional instructions which you should carefully and strictly follow during your deliberations.

1. Do not let bias, prejudice or sympathy play any part in your deliberations.
2. In arriving at your answers, consider only the evidence introduced here under oath and such exhibits, if any, as have been introduced for your consideration under the rulings of the Court; that is, what you have seen and heard in this courtroom, together with the law as given you by the court. In your deliberations, you will not consider or discuss anything that is not represented by the evidence in this case.
3. Since every answer that is required by the charge is important, no juror should state or consider that any required answer is not important.
4. You must not decide who you think should win, and then try to answer the questions accordingly. Simply answer the questions, and do not discuss nor concern yourselves with the effect of your answers.
5. You will not decide an issue by lot or by drawing straws, or by any other method of chance. Do not render a quotient verdict. A quotient verdict means that the jurors agree to abide by the result to be reached by adding together each juror's figure and dividing by the number of jurors to get an average. Do not do any trading on your answers; that is, one juror should not agree to answer a certain question one way if others will agree to answer another question another way.
6. Your verdict must be unanimous and must be signed by your foreperson.

These instructions are given you because your conduct is subject to review the same as that of the witnesses, parties, attorneys and the judge. If it should be found that you have disregarded any of these instructions, it will be jury misconduct and it may require another trial by another jury; then all of our time will have been wasted.

The foreperson or any other juror who observes a violation of the court's instructions shall immediately warn the one who is violating the same and caution the juror not to do so again.

By the term "preponderance of the evidence," as used in this charge, is meant the greater weight and degree of credible evidence before you.

By the term "negligence," as used in this charge, is meant a failure to do that which a person of ordinary prudence, in the exercise of ordinary care, would do under the same or similar circumstances, or the doing of that which a person of ordinary prudence, in the exercise of ordinary care, would not do under the same or similar circumstances.

By the term "ordinary care" is meant that degree of care which would be exercised by a person of ordinary care and prudence under the same or similar circumstances.

By the term "proximate cause," as used in this charge, is meant a cause which in a natural and continuous sequence, produces an event and without which the event would not have occurred; and to be a proximate cause of an event, it should have reasonably anticipated and foreseen by a person of ordinary care and prudence, in the exercise of ordinary care, that the event or some similar event would occur as a natural and probable consequence. There may be more than one proximate cause of an event.

SPECIAL INTERROGATORY NO. 1

Do you find from a preponderance of the evidence that the carts supplied on the occasion in question by Defendant, its agents or employees, were bent and defective?

Answer "We do" or "We do not."

ANSWER: _We do_

If you have answered Special Interrogatory No. 1 "We do," and only in that event, then answer:

SPECIAL INTERROGATORY NO. 2

Do you find from a preponderance of the evidence that such conduct, if any you have found, was negligent?

Answer "We do" or "We do not."

ANSWER: _We do_

If you have answered Special Interrogatory No. 2 "We do," and only in that event, then answer:

SPECIAL INTERROGATORY NO. 3

Do you find from a preponderance of the evidence that such negligence, if any you have found, was a proximate cause of the occurrence in question?

Answer "We do" or "We do not."

ANSWER: _We do_

SPECIAL INTERROGATORY NO. 4

Do you find from a preponderance of the evidence that in pulling on the carts in question, Miranda Dominguez failed to keep such a lookout for her safety as would a person in the exercise of ordinary care?

Answer "We do" or "We do not."

ANSWER: _We do not_

SPECIAL INTERROGATORY NO. 5

Do you find from a preponderance of the evidence that such failure, if any, was a proximate cause of the occurrence in question?

Answer "We do" or "We do not."

ANSWER: _____

SPECIAL INTERROGATORY NO. 6

Do you find from a preponderance of the evidence that Miranda Dominguez pulled on the cart in such a manner as would not have been done by a person in the exercise of ordinary care?

Answer "We do" or "We do not."

ANSWER: *We do not*

If you have answered Special Interrogatory No. 6 "We do," and only in that event, then answer:

SPECIAL INTERROGATORY NO. 7

Do you find from a preponderance of the evidence that Miranda Dominguez's conduct in pulling on the bascart was a proximate cause of the occurrence in question?

Answer "We do" or "We do not."

ANSWER: _____

SPECIAL INTERROGATORY NO. 8

What sum of money, if any, if paid now in cash, do you find from a preponderance of this evidence would fairly and reasonably compensate Miranda Dominguez for her injuries, if any, which you find from a preponderance of the evidence resulted from the occurrences in question?

You may consider the following elements of damage, if any, and none other:
a. Physical pain and mental anguish in the past.
b. Physical pain and mental anguish which, in reasonable probability, she will suffer in the future.

Answer in dollars and cents, if any.

ANSWER: *$6500.00 (Sixty-five hundred dollars)*

After you retire to the jury room you will select your own foreperson. The first thing the foreperson will do is to have this complete charge read aloud and then you will deliberate upon your answers to the questions asked.

John T. Hughes
Judge Presiding

CERTIFICATE

We, the jury, have answered the above and foregoing special issues as herein indicated, and herewith return same into court as our verdict.

(To be signed by the foreperson.)

Philip R. Cortelli
Foreperson

J. OBJECTIONS TO THE CHARGE

101

Comes now the Defendant at the conclusion of the evidence in the case and after the preparation of the Court's Charge but before retirement of the jury and, in the presence of and with the consent of the Court and opposing counsel, makes the following objections and exceptions to the Court's Charge by dictating same to the Court Reporter, * * *

The Defendant objects to Special Interrogatory No. 1 for the following reasons:

(a.) There is no evidence to support the submission thereof or any finding by the jury based thereon.

(b.) There is insufficient evidence to support the submission to the jury thereof or any finding based thereon.

(c.) There are no pleadings to support said issue.

(d.) It assumes a disputed conclusion, namely, that if there was a defect in the carts causing them to stick, such defect was attributable to action or inaction of Defendant; and it fails to inquire of any causal act of Defendant.

(Livingston's objections to the charge consume seven pages of the record and attack all of plaintiff's interrogatories as well as certain definitions. Note that Fed. R. Civ. P. 51 provides that a defect in the charge must be objected to before the jury retires; the objections are intended to preserve error for appeal. Livingston concludes thus * * *):

Defendant objects to the Court's failure to charge, as requested by Defendant, upon the law of unavoidable accident as that term is understood in the law of West York, or to instruct the jury that "an event may be an unavoidable accident, that is, an accident not proximately caused by the negligence of either party," or words to substantially similar effect.

THE COURT: The court having considered Defendant's objections to the charge, they are in all things overruled.

K. NOTES AND QUESTIONS ON COURT'S CHARGE, OBJECTIONS, AND JURY ARGUMENT

1. GENERAL CHARGE, SPECIAL INTERROGATORIES OR BOTH? Rule 49 affords the trial judge discretion in choosing a general charge (consisting of instruction on the law, plus a verdict for plaintiff or defendant) or special interrogatories (consisting of questions on the fact issues). Special interrogatories are thought to have the advantage that they control the jury, require a verdict in accordance with the law and evidence more rigorously than the general charge, and provide reviewable findings. However, special interrogatories depend heavily upon precision of language and careful drafting. Breaking down a claim into its consistuent elements, and formulating them in an intelligible way, is not always feasible. The general charge is often considered to have the advantages of avoiding violation of common sense and of permitting the jury's traditional function of rounding the rough edges of the law.

2. STRUCTURE OF THE CHARGE. A charge using special interrogatories, such as this charge, generally consists of three types of elements. First, there are general instructions (regarding such matters as election of a foreperson). Secondly, there are definitions of legal principles applicable to the specific type of case being tried (negligence, proximate causation, preponderance of the evidence). Finally, there are the special interrogatories themselves, accompanied by verdict forms.

3. DRAFTING OF THE CHARGE; STRATEGY. The court frequently prepares the charge from submissions by the attorneys. At the conclusion of all the evidence, the judge will generally recess the jury

and retire to chambers with the attorneys to discuss the charge. In this case, the judge has adopted substantially the submissions made by the attorneys for their respective liability issues; notice the strategy involved. For example, the contributory negligence issues (which were submitted by defendant) ask whether the plaintiff failed to exercise "ordinary care." Is this wording less harsh, and therefore more likely to produce a positive answer, than plaintiff's wording, which asks whether defendant was "negligent?"

4. OBJECTIONS. Rule 51 provides that errors in the charge are not reversible unless objected to (the contemporaneous objection rule is a general rule, not applicable only to charge matters). Therefore, charge objections are frequently detailed, and indeed in the real case from which these materials are taken, owing to technical requirements, they were more voluminous than is indicated here.

5. ORDER OF CHARGE AND ARGUMENT. Rule 51 provides that the court's charge follows the jury arguments, somewhat placing the cart before the horse. It is difficult for attorneys to argue intelligently unless they know the content of the charge. For this reason, the rule also requires the court to notify the attorneys concerning its ruling on each requested charge.

Incidentally, a written charge is not required, and some courts charge the jury orally. In the Middle District of West York, the practice is to charge the jury in writing and to permit the jury to take the written charge to the deliberation room.

6. JURY ARGUMENT. To a skillful attorney, argument is very important. It is the attorney's opportunity to illustrate the significance of the evidence, which may have been presented in disjointed bits and pieces. Furthermore, it is the attorney's opportunity to persuade the jury of the desired conclusions from the evidence, and to put the evidence together with an explanation of the often-confusing legal terms in a court's charge. Thus the correlation of raw evidence, reasonable inferences, and legal standards is the function of jury argument. In addition, jury argument frequently contains an important emotional content. Although controversial, this element is essential, because most legal conceptions (e.g., "ordinary care") express, at their core, fundamental societal values, which cannot be effectively explored without emotional argument. Thus defendant will extol the interest of a storekeeper in running a business without unduly burdensome obligations, and plaintiff will argue the right of an elderly consumer to expect safe equipment.

7. THE STRUCTURE OF JURY ARGUMENT. Plaintiff, having the burden of proof, is accorded the right to open and close the argument. (What advantages are given plaintiff by the right of rebuttal?) It is typical for the plaintiff to open with a short introduction praising the jury system, followed by explanation of the definitions and instructions in the charge, followed by an analysis of the special interrogatories and a marshalling of the evidence to produce the desired result in each. An effective defense argument will rebut a select few points made by the plaintiff (only a few, to avoid having plaintiff's counsel dictate the defense argument), and then will proceed to explain the charge, marshal the evidence from the defendant's view on each special issue, advocate the conclusion desired by defendant on each, and give the jury the emotional basis for the holding. Plaintiff's rebuttal argument reiterates the major points made in opening—and then, typically, unleashes the plaintiff's most powerful emotional basis for the desired holding. See whether you can determine the extent to which the parties have followed this argument pattern in the present case, and consider what difference in argument technique would be exhibited if a general charge, rather than special interrogatories, were used.

8. VERDICT. In the real case, state law allowed a non-unanimous verdict, rendered by 10 or more of the 12 jury members. The jury was, in fact, non-unanimous—with the dissenters reflecting the weakness of plaintiff's evidence. In federal courts, a unanimous verdict is required.

CHAPTER SIX:

THE POST-TRIAL STAGE AND THE APPEAL

A. JUDGMENT AND POST-TRIAL MOTIONS

NOTE ON RECEIPT OF VERDICT, MOTION FOR JUDGMENT, AND ENTRY OF JUDGMENT

When the jury returned its special verdicts, the trial judge read the jury's answers to the interrogatories submitted to it, in open court. He asked whether there were any objections to irregularities in the special verdicts. Hearing none, the judge stated, "The verdict is received."

Mr. Elder then moved for judgment. He did so by simply saying, "The Plaintiff moves for judgment on the jury's verdict."

The court granted Plaintiff's motion and directed plaintiff to prepare, serve on defendant, and file a proposed form of judgment. Defendant was directed to serve and file objections, if any, within three days after receipt. Both parties approved the judgment as to form, and it was signed and entered by the court as follows:

JUDGMENT

```
        IN THE UNITED STATES DISTRICT COURT
        FOR THE MIDDLE DISTRICT OF WEST YORK
                 LONDON DIVISION


MIRANDA DOMINGUEZ, Plaintiff          )
v.                                    )    NO. CA-71-4683
SCOTT'S FOOD STORES, INC., Defendant  )

                    JUDGMENT
     Be it remembered that on the 18th day of September, 2000,
came on for trial the above entitled and numbered cause, wherein
Miranda Dominguez is Plaintiff and Scott's Food Stores, Inc. is
Defendant, and came all parties to such cause, and presented
their evidence to a jury, and the jury having rendered its answers
```

upon special interrogatories, and the Plaintiff having made and the Court having duly heard and considered a Motion for Judgment, and such additional considerations and findings as were authorized by law having been had and made, and the Court being of the opinion that judgment should be rendered for Plaintiff Miranda Dominguez, it is therefore:

Ordered, adjudged and decreed by the Court that the said Plaintiff, Miranda Dominguez do have and recover of and from Defendant Scott's Food Stores, Inc. the sum of SIX THOUSAND FIVE HUNDRED AND NO/100 ($6,500.00) DOLLARS, together with costs and interest thereon from the date of judgment.

Signed and entered this the ___*19*___ day of ___*September*___, 2000.

MOTION FOR JUDGMENT AS A MATTER OF LAW

IN THE UNITED STATES DISTRICT COURT
FOR THE MIDDLE DISTRICT OF WEST YORK
LONDON DIVISION

MIRANDA DOMINGUEZ, Plaintiff	)	
v.	)	NO. CA-71-4683
SCOTT'S FOOD STORES, INC., Defendant	)	

DEFENDANT'S MOTION FOR JUDGMENT
AS A MATTER OF LAW

Comes now, Scott's Food Stores, Inc., Defendant in the above styled and numbered cause, and files this its Motion for Judgment as a Matter of Law, having previously made a motion for directed verdict at the close of all the evidence, and moves the Court to set aside the judgment heretofore rendered, and to render judgment for Defendant, for the following reasons:

1. The jury's answer of "we do" in response to special interrogatories numbers 1, 2 and 3, and to each of such special interrogatories, were supported by legally insufficient evidence.

2. As a matter of law, Plaintiff's evidence failed to support any reasonable conclusion, by a preponderance of the evidence, that the carts in question, alleged to have injured Plaintiff, were bent and defective, as found by the jury; or that any act of negligence was committed by Defendant, as found by the jury; or that any such act was a proximate cause of Plaintiff's injuries, as found by the jury.

For these reasons, Defendant prays that Plaintiff take nothing, and that Defendant recover its costs.

Respectfully submitted,

MCINTOSH & WALKER

By: *Robert L. Livingston Jr*
Robert L. Livingston, Jr.
First National Bank Building
London, West York 77002

MOTION FOR NEW TRIAL

IN THE UNITED STATES DISTRICT COURT
FOR THE MIDDLE DISTRICT OF WEST YORK
LONDON DIVISION

MIRANDA DOMINGUEZ, Plaintiff)
v.) NO. CA-71-4683
SCOTT'S FOOD STORES, INC., Defendant)

DEFENDANT'S MOTION FOR NEW TRIAL

Comes now, Scott's Food Stores, Inc., Defendant in the above styled and numbered cause, and files this its Motion for New Trial, and moves the Court to set aside the Judgment heretofore rendered against this Defendant and to grant a new trial for each of the following good and sufficient reasons:

1. The Court should grant Defendant's Motion for New Trial in that the jury's affirmative answers to special interrogatories numbers 1, 2, and 3, and each of them, are not supported by sufficient evidence, and are against the great weight and preponderance of the evidence.

2. The Court should grant Defendant's Motion for New Trial in that the jury's negative answers to special issues numbers 4 and 6, and each of them, are against the great weight of the evidence. The jury's consequent failure to answer special interrogatories numbers 5 and 7 was caused by such findings against the great weight of the evidence.

3. The Court should grant Defendant's Motion for New Trial in that the jury's affirmative answer to special issue number 8, concerning damages, is shown by the great weight of the evidence to be excessive.

4. The Court erred in allowing repetitious questioning of Plaintiff, and repetitious answers by Plaintiff, concerning her inspection of the carts in question, over the Defendant's objection.

5. The Court erred in refusing, over objection, to instruct the jury in accordance with Defendant's requested instruction on the legal principle of "unavoidable accident" as that term is defined in the law of West York, and in failing to instruct the jury that "an event may be an unavoidable accident, that is, an accident not proximately caused by the negligence of either party," or words to substantially similar effect.

For these reasons, Defendant prays that the Court set aside the judgment heretofore rendered against this Defendant and that a new trial be granted.

Respectfully submitted,

MCINTOSH & WALKER

By: _Robert L. Livingston Jr._
Robert L. Livingston, Jr.
First City National Bank Building
London, West York 77002

B. THE TAKING OF THE APPEAL

ROBERT LIVINGSTON'S MEMORANDUM TO THE FILE CONCERNING TIME SCHEDULE ON APPEAL

(1) Judgment: Entered September 19, 2000

(2) Post-Trial Motions: Due--September 29, 2000. Filed. Overruled: November 20, 2000. Fed. R. Civ. P. 50(b), 59(b).

(3) Notice of Appeal: Due 30 days after entry of order denying motions (December 20, 2000). Filed--December 12, 2000. Required by Fed. R. App. P. 3(a), 4(a)(4).

(4) Cost Bond: Due same date as Notice of Appeal. Filed December 12, 2000. Fed. R. App. P. 7; Local District Court Rules.

(5) Ordering of Transcript: Must be ordered within 10 days after notice of appeal. Required, December 22, 2000. Ordered: November 20, 2000. Fed. R. App. P. 10. Ordered from reporter.

(6) Appellant's Brief: Due within 40 days after the date of filing of the record. (Appellee's Brief due 30 days thereafter, and reply brief 14 days thereafter). Fed. R. App. P. 31.

(7) Payment of Fees: Due--$25.00 at the time of filing of Notice of Appeal. Fed. R. App. P. 3(e).

(8) Petition for Rehearing: Due 14 days after Appellate Court Judgment. Fed. R. App. P. 40.

(9) Stay of Mandate: Mandate issues 21 days after judgment, but can be stayed for a period of 30 days. Fed. R. App. P. 41.

(10) Petition for Certiorari: Due 45 days after final judgment. Supreme Court Rule 22(3).

Permission to appeal has been sought from the client by letter separately contained in this file, explaining probable costs of $2-5,000, chances of less than 50-50 but substantial, and explaining grounds of appeal as contained in Motion for New Trial. Received this day, December 1, 2000, permission from Mr. Tom Ball, acting on behalf of Scott's Food Stores, Inc., to undertake the appeal. (See letter from Tom Ball in file).

MODIFICATION OF PLAINTIFF'S FEE CONTRACT

June 3, 2001

Mr. Steve Elder
Attorney at Law
Suite 412
First Savings Building
London, West York 77002

RE: 16312, Scott's Food Stores, Inc. v. Miranda Dominguez

Dear Mr. Elder:

This letter confirms our agreement that your fee for the appeal of this case will be an additional 10% of the total recovery.

Sincerely,

Miranda Dominguez
Miranda Dominguez

REQUESTS FOR PREPARATION OF RECORD

ROBERT L. LIVINGSTON, JR.
McINTOSH & WALKER
FIRST CITY NATIONAL BANK BUILDING
LONDON, WEST YORK 77002

November 20, 2000

Miss Ann Vernon
Reporter
District Court
Federal Building
London, West York 77002

Re: No. CA-71-4683
     Miranda Dominguez vs.
     Scott's Food Stores, Inc.
Dear Miss Vernon: District Court

Defendant, Scott's Food Stores, Inc., desires to appeal from the judgment of the Trial Court in the captioned cause. Please prepare in question and answer form a transcript of all proceedings before the court, including Motions for Directed Verdict, both when Plaintiff rested her case and when both sides had rested their causes. You have already prepared my Objections and Exceptions to the Court's Charge which will be forwarded to the Court for his signature to be placed in the file.

Very truly yours,

MCINTOSH & WALKER

By *Robert L. Livingston, Jr.*
   Robert L. Livingston, Jr.

ROBERT L. LIVINGSTON, JR.
McINTOSH & WALKER
FIRST CITY NATIONAL BANK BUILDING
LONDON, WEST YORK 77002

David Webster, District Clerk
Federal Building
London, West York 77002
                                    November 20, 2000

Attn: Mr. John Thomas
       Chief Deputy

                              Re: No. CA-71-4683 - Miranda
                                   Dominguez vs. Scott's Food
                                   Stores, Inc. - In the
                                   District Court

Dear Sir:

     Please include the following in the record in the above
entitled and numbered cause:
     (1) Plaintiff's First Amended Complaint;
     (2) Defendant's Answer;
     (3) Charge of the Court and jury's answers thereto;
     (4) Defendant's Objections and Exceptions to the Court's
     Charge;
     (5) Judgment of the Court;
     (6) Defendant's Motion for Judgment Notwithstanding the
     Verdict;
     (7) Defendant's Motion for New Trial;
     (8) Order Overruling Defendant's Motion for New Trial and
     Motion for Judgment Notwithstanding the Verdict;
     (9) Notice of Appeal;
    (10) Letter of this date to Court Reporter requesting
    preparation of transcript;
    (11) Cost Bond on Appeal;
    (12) Copy of this designation of items to be included
    in the record.

     Thank you for your assistance in this matter.

                              Very truly yours,

                              MCINTOSH & WALKER

                              By Robert L. Livingston, Jr.
                                  Robert L. Livingston, Jr.

ORDER OVERRULING POST-TRIAL MOTIONS

IN THE UNITED STATES DISTRICT COURT
FOR THE MIDDLE DISTRICT OF WEST YORK
LONDON DIVISION

MIRANDA DOMINGUEZ, Plaintiff   )
v.   )   NO. CA-71-4683
SCOTT'S FOOD STORES, INC., Defendant)

ORDER

Came on to be heard this day Defendant's Motion for Judgment Notwithstanding the Verdict and Motion for New Trial, and the Court having considered the same, Defendant's Motion for Judgment Notwithstanding the Verdict and Motion for New Trial are hereby in all things overruled.

Entered this 20th day of November, 2000.

John T. Hughes
<u>United States District Judge</u>

NOTICE OF APPEAL

IN THE UNITED STATES DISTRICT COURT
FOR THE MIDDLE DISTRICT OF WEST YORK
LONDON DIVISION

MIRANDA DOMINGUEZ, Plaintiff   )
v.   )   NO. CA-71-4683
SCOTT'S FOOD STORES, INC., Defendant)

NOTICE OF APPEAL

Notice is hereby given that Scott's Food Stores, Inc., Defendant above named, hereby appeals to the United States Court of Appeals for the Fourteenth Circuit from the final judgment entered in this action on the 19th day of September, 2000.

Respectfully submitted,

MCINTOSH & WALKER

By: _Robert L. Livingston Jr._
<u>Robert L. Livingston, Jr.</u>
McIntosh & Walker
First City National Bank Bldg.
London, West York 77002

COST BOND

<u>COST BOND ON APPEAL</u>

WHEREAS, in cause no. CA-71-4683, Miranda Dominguez v. Scott's Food Stores, Inc., in the United States District Court for the Middle District of West York, London Division, at a regular term of said court, to-wit on the 19th day of September, 1973, Miranda Dominguez recovered of and from the Defendant, Scott's Food Stores, Inc., the sum of $6,500.00, together with interest at the rate of 6% per annum from date of judgment until paid, from which judgment Scott's Food Stores, Inc., desires to take an appeal to the Court of Appeals for the Fourteenth Circuit, sitting at London, West York;

NOW, THEREFORE, KNOW ALL MEN BY THESE PERSONS that Scott's Food Stores, Inc., as Principal, and WEST YORK GENERAL INSURANCE COMPANY, as Surety, acknowledge ourselves bound to pay unto the said David Webster, District Clerk, the sum of $500.00, less such sums as may have been paid by Appellant on the costs, conditioned that Appellant shall prosecute its appeal with effect, and shall pay all costs which have accrued in the Trial Court and the cost of the record.

WITNESS OUR HANDS on this 5th day of December, 2000.

Scott's Food Stores, Inc.

By _Tom E. Ball_____
           Principal

WEST YORK GENERAL INSURANCE COMPANY

BY _Jane Pryor_____
           Surety
Jane Pryor   Attorney-in-Fact

(There are two pages attached to the bond. One contains the clerk's estimate of cost of preparing the record on appeal at $1000. The other contains a certified copy of West York General's appointment of Jane Pryor as its attorney-in-fact to make bonds of this type.)

EXCERPTS FROM APPELLANT'S BRIEF

NO. 75-1111
IN THE UNITED STATES COURT OF APPEALS
FOR THE FOURTEENTH CIRCUIT

SCOTT'S FOOD STORES, INC.
V.
MIRANDA DOMINGUEZ

ON APPEAL FROM THE UNITED STATES DIS-
TRICT COURT FOR THE MIDDLE DISTRICT
OF WEST YORK, LONDON DIVISION

BRIEF OF APPELLANT

ISSUES PRESENTED

1. Whether the district court erred in overruling Defendant's Motion for Directed Verdict and Motion for Judgment Notwithstanding the Verdict.

2. Whether the district court abused its discretion in denying Defendant a new trial because the verdict was against the great weight of the evidence.

3. Whether the district court erred in repeatedly allowing a witness, Mrs. Miranda Dominguez, to respond to questions to which she had previously responded, over the timely and proper objection of this appellant that such testimony was repetitious.

STATEMENT OF THE CASE

This is a suit arising out of bodily injuries allegedly sustained by Mrs. Miranda Dominguez, hereinafter referred to as "appellee," or "plaintiff," when she attempted to pull a shopping cart out of a cluster of shopping carts which were nested together and was pushed backward by a grouping of three or four nested shopping carts which dislodged from the larger cluster together, thus causing her to fall.

Appellant takes the position in this appeal that the evidence was legally insufficient to support submission to the jury of special interrogatories one through three in that there was no evidence that the carts which allegedly caused appellee's injury were "bent and defective," or that appellant was negligent, or that any such negligence was a proximate cause of appellee's injuries. Appellant contends that even should this Honorable Court conclude that there was sufficient evidence to support such submission of the special interrogatories to the jury, which appellant insistently denies, a review of the whole record before the court will reveal that the judgment must be reversed and remanded for a new trial in that the result is so against the great weight and preponderance of the evidence that the lower court's denial of a new trial on this ground was an abuse of discretion. Appellant contends that the lower court also erred in allowing counsel for appellee, over the objection of counsel for appellant, to question his own witness in a highly repetitious manner.

SUMMARY OF ARGUMENT

Defendant was entitled to a directed verdict and to a judgment notwithstanding the verdict because no legally cognizable evidence supported the jury's findings that defendant's carts, upon which plaintiff pulled, were "bent and defective," or that defendant was negligent with respect thereto, or that any such negligence was a proximate cause of the incident. Plaintiff testified that she "did not notice" whether the carts were bent or defective. No other witness testified to the condition of the carts in question. Plaintiff did introduce some evidence by which she charged that other carts, on other occasions, may have been rusty, bent, or mistreated by third persons unknown. That evidence, however, did not relate to the carts here in question and established nothing with respect to them. To support submission of a question to a jury, a plaintiff's proof must be such that it would enable a reasonable person to conclude that the greater weight of the evidence indicates the facts claimed by plaintiff. If the evidence supports other hypotheses equally well, so that no reasonable person could say that the greater weight supports plaintiff's hypothesis, a directed verdict is required. E.g., Pennsylvania R. Co. v. Chamberlain, 228 U.S. 333 (1933).

(The remainder of the summary of argument is omitted.)

ARGUMENT

I. DEFENDANT WAS ENTITLED TO A DIRECTED VERDICT OR TO A
JUDGMENT NOTWITHSTANDING THE VERDICT BECAUSE PLAINTIFF
INTRODUCED NO EVIDENCE FROM WHICH THE JURY COULD HAVE REASONABLY
INFERRED THAT DEFENDANT'S CARTS WERE "BENT AND DEFECTIVE," OR
THAT DEFENDANT WAS NEGLIGENT WITH RESPECT TO THE CARTS, OR THAT
ANY SUCH NEGLIGENCE PROXIMATELY CAUSED THE INCIDENT.

It is the contention of this appellant that the evidence supporting the jury's finding on Special Interrogatories 2 and 3 -- that the carts in question were bent and defective, that defendant was negligent, and that such negligence was a proximate cause of plaintiff's injuries -- was of such slight probative value as to amount only to surmise or suspicion. Under the established test for legal sufficiency, slight evidence such as this amounts to no evidence.

The sum total of direct testimony with regard to whether the bascarts in question were bent or defective is as follows:

Mr. Dominguez, the husband of appellee and the first witness to appear at the trial below, testified in response to the questions by appellee's (plaintiff's below) counsel as follows (R 39):

Q Now, you did not go up and inspect the cart or carts that your wife might have been pushed down by?
A No.

The only other testimony elicited from Mr. Dominguez relating to the bascarts was as follows (R 39):

Q Did you ever see the carts left out in the parking lot?
A Oh, yes.
Q Did you ever see any carts that were used by people to carry groceries home as they walked home?
A Yes.
Q Did you ever see them left out in the rain?
A Yes.
Q Did you ever see them lying on their side?
A Yes.
Q Have you ever seen children playing in the carts?
A Yes, many times.

This testimony relates to unidentified bascarts at some time prior to the day of the accident in question. It sheds absolutely no light on the condition of the bascarts which were involved in the injuries to plaintiff. Neither does it tend to establish, even inferentially, that these bascarts on the occasion in question were bent and defective, for such an inference would be improper because a transitory condition can not logically be established by evidence of a condition on prior occasions.

Mrs. Dominguez, the appellee herein, on direct examination by her attorney testified as follows (R 59):

Q At the time you were in the store on the day that you were injured, Mrs. Dominguez, did you make any observation about the shopping carts?
A No.
Q Did you make any observation about the condition of the shopping carts when you were in there? * * *
A Well, I never had seen the baskets being repaired or nothing. * * *

Q I am not asking you whether you ever saw them repaired. I am asking you, did you see the condition of them when you went into the store?
A Yes. They looked pretty old already.
Q Did any of them appear rusty?
A Yes.
Q Did any of them appear to be bent?
A Yes, sir.
Q Did any of the wheels ever not turn or would not go straight?

(At this point counsel for appellant lodged an objection if counsel was speaking of any other day than the day of the accident, which objection was sustained by the court.)

Counsel for appellee then withdrew the question and continued as follows (R 61):

Q Did you ever notice that any of the tubular frames were bent on this day?
A No. I did not notice that.

Any probative value of the above colloquy as it reflects on the bent or defective condition of the bascarts in question on the day in question is vitiated by the witness's contradictory testimony. Mrs. Dominguez first testified on direct examination that she had not made any observation about the shopping carts. Her counsel, in a deliberate attempt to impeach or resurrect his own witness, persisted in coaxing her to contradict her prior testimony. Momemtarily successful in eliciting the response from Mrs. Dominguez that the bascarts "appeared to be bent," practically in the next breath Mrs. Dominguez testified that she "did not notice" whether any of the tubular frames were bent on the day of the accident.

<The brief quotes further from the record, showing statements of plaintiff to the effect that she did not look at the baskets, but "just grabbed one," that she did not "glance at them;" and that she did not "look at them at all." The brief also summarizes the evidence regarding bent and rusty carts and shows that all such references were to other carts, on other occasions. It then continues as follows:>

That it was a bent or defective cart that allegedly caused plaintiff's injury is within the realm of pure speculation. Just as easily, the carts could have been stuck together because of a popsicle stick placed or dropped between the grating on one of the carts by a customer's child. Ms. Dominguez herself admitted that sticking "is just something carts do." The accident may have been occasioned by Ms. Dominguez' pulling too hard on the cart she wanted or pulling it at an improper angle. There are numerous other possibilities.

As the Supreme Court said in Pennsylvania R. Co. v. Chamberlain, 288 U.S. 333, 339 (1933),

* * * At most, there was an inference to that effect drawn from observed facts which gave equal support to the opposite inference * * *.

We, therefore, have a case belonging to that class of cases where proven facts given equal support to each of two inconsistent inferences; in which event, neither of them being established, judgment, as a matter of law, must go against the party upon whom rests the necessity of sustaining one of these inferences as against the other, before he is entitled to judgment.

Ms. Dominguez's evidence fits this description exactly. Another way to view the legal test is that the proof must be such that it would allow a reasonable person—perhaps not every reasonable person, but some reasonable person—to conclude that the preponderance of the evidence supports the proposition argued by the party with the burden of persuasion (here the plaintiff). See Trawick v. Manhattan Life Ins. Co., 447 F 2d 1293 (5th Cir. 1971); Mattivi v. South African Marine Corp., 618 F. 2d 163, 167 (2d Cir. 1980); 9C. Wright and A. Miller, Federal Practice and Procedure sec. 2524 (1971 and West Supp. 1983). Plaintiff's proof in this case does not meet that test, and judgment should have been rendered for defendant.

II. DEFENDANT WAS ENTITLED TO A NEW TRIAL BECAUSE THE JURY'S ANSWERS TO THE LIABILITY ISSUES WERE AGAINST THE GREAT WEIGHT OF THE EVIDENCE

⟨The remainder of the brief, dealing with the second and third issues raised by defendant, is omitted.⟩

NOTE ON PLAINTIFF'S BRIEF

Plaintiff's brief responded to this argument by pointing out that a heavy burden was on defendant to show that no reasonable inference supported the verdict. Plaintiff also pointed out that the testimony included several instances in which plaintiff described the carts, that crediting that testimony was within the province of the jury, and that the jury was entitled to discard contrary testimony or inferences. Additionally, the brief cited cases holding that circumstantial evidence (such as the condition of other carts on other days) could be used to support a reasonable inference that defective carts proximately cause the injury. Finally, plaintiff relied heavily upon the testimony of defendant's own witnesses, who testified that it was "very, very possible" that the incident could have happened because the carts were defective.

C. NOTES AND QUESTIONS REGARDING POST-TRIAL MOTIONS AND APPEAL

1. POST-TRIAL MOTIONS. Identify the respective functions of the post-trial motions. Under Rules 50 and 59, is defendant entitled to the relief requested?

2. PERFECTING THE APPEAL; SCHEDULING. Perfection of an appeal requires the satisfaction of certain requirements—including notice of appeal, filing of a cost bond, preparation and filing of the record (which appellant must arrange with the clerk and court reporter), and filing of Appellant's brief, in addition to requirements imposed by the local rules of the particular appellate court. Each requirement is subject to a time limit. A careful attorney prepares a time schedule at the commencement of the appeal to ensure that he complies with time requirements. See Federal Rules of Appellate Procedure 3, 4, 7, 10-12, 31.

3. APPELLANT'S BRIEF. The required contents of appellant's brief, and format requirements, are set out by federal rules of appellate procedure 28.

4. DISPOSITION OF THE APPEAL. Is defendant's argument well taken, given the evidence submitted?

5. ORAL ARGUMENT ON APPEAL. Many appellate courts consider oral argument less important than is popularly supposed, and the court of appeals in this case invoked a local rule enabling it to determine the case on briefs alone. (In the real case, the court was required by law to receive oral argument.) The court's opinion follows.

D. THE APPELLATE COURT'S DECISION

APPELLATE OPINION

SCOTT'S FOOD STORE
V.
MIRANDA DOMINGUEZ,
OCT. 10, 2001

EVERETT, Circuit Justice.

Ms. Miranda Dominguez recovered judgment on a jury verdict against Scott's in the amount of $6,500.00 as damages for injury sustained in one of Scott's retail grocery stores. We affirm.

Ms. Miranda Dominguez fell, suffering a broken wrist, when she pulled on a shopping cart in Scott's No. 14 grocery store. Ms. Dominguez testified that when she pulled on the shopping cart basket, the whole row of carts (called "bascarts") came toward her causing her to fall on her right hand. The jury found that the bascarts were bent and defective; that this was a dangerous condition maintained by Scott's which knew or should have known the condition; and that Scott's was negligent in failing to repair or replace the bascarts. The jury also answered the causation issue in favor of Ms. Dominguez and refused to find that she had failed to keep a proper lookout or that she had pulled on the bascart in such a manner as would not have been done by a person in the exercise of ordinary care.

In its points of error, Scott's attacks the legal and factual sufficiency of the evidence on questions of primary negligence and proximate cause.

Basically Scott's position is that there is no evidence in the record from which the jury could properly have inferred that the particular bascarts involved in Ms. Dominguez's accident were bent and defective.

Mr. Dominguez testified that he drove his wife to the Scott's No. 14 store on the evening in question so that she could buy groceries. They lived about four or five blocks from the store and bought groceries there every week. Mr. Dominguez usually stayed in the car while his wife shopped and when she had completed her shopping he would go in and help her with the groceries. Shortly after Ms. Dominguez went into the store on the day in question, a lady came running out and told Mr. Dominguez that his wife had fallen down.

Ms. Dominguez testified that she walked into the store and reached for a bascart with her right hand. She said the baskets were of the type that the basket flips up and the other basket moved in behind it; that there was a row of approximately 50 bascarts nested together. She said when she pulled on the bascart the whole row of bascarts came toward her causing her to fall. She said there must have been about five or six bascarts out of the big stack that came toward her and they caused her to lose her balance, pushing her to the floor. She said she made no inspection of the baskets and just walked up and pulled on the first basket in line. She said when she pulled on the basket all the bascarts came toward her and threw her to the floor. She said "I pull light but they were all stuck together." She said she had had a basket stick before, but did not know that "the whole thing would come toward me."

116

Scott's argues that the record is silent as to any direct evidence of the condition of the bascarts in question at the time of the occurrence. It contends that Ms. Dominguez's testimony shows she did not inspect or even observe the particular bascarts which were involved in the injury and that her testimony is contradictory as to the extent of her observation on that date. Scott's further contends the trial court erred in permitting Ms. Dominguez to state, over objection, that she had observed the condition of the bascarts, after earlier testifying that she had not made an observation about the bascarts on the date that she was injured.

Ms. Dominguez testified that when she pulled upon the bascart it stuck together with five or six others and that all came together at her in a bunch, causing her to fall to the floor. Scott's shop dispatcher and maintenance man testifed that it was "very, very possible" that several bascarts nested in a row would stick together if they were bent. Scott's property accountant testified that the bascarts were repaired in their shop so that they would be "easy to push in the store." He admitted knowledge that the purpose of such repair was to avoid having the bascarts stick together and come toward a customer in a bunch when one bascart was pulled loose.

The circumstances in which an injury occurred may sometimes afford proof of the act or condition which caused the injury. Lavender v. Kurn, 327 U.S. 645 (1946). The jury was at liberty to conclude from Ms. Dominguez's testimony describing the manner in which the accident occurred and the testimony of Scott's employees, which tended to show how the occurrence could likely have happened, that the injury was caused by the bent and defective condition of one or more of the bascarts in question.

That there might be more than one reason why the bascarts would stick and come together in a bunch does not necessitate a conclusion that the evidence was legally insufficient to support the jury's verdict. Lavender v. Kurn, supra. Ms. Dominguez was not required to exclude every other possible cause of the occurrence.

Scott's managed the store in question and furnished the bascarts to its customers for their use and convenience while shopping at its store. It assumed exclusive responsibility for the maintenance and repair of its bascarts and if the occurrence was the result of some cause other than their defective condition, Scott's had the means and opportunity to ascertain that fact and make appropriate explanation. (Citations ommited.) There is no suggestion in the record as to any cause of the accident other than that offered by Scott's employees which tended to show the cause to have been the defective condition of one or more of the bascarts.

In addition to the evidence discussed above as to the circumstances surrounding the accident, the jury heard testimony from which they could have concluded that the bascarts in Scott's No. 14 store were generally in bad condition and needed repair at the time of Ms. Dominguez's injury. Ms. Dominguez's husband testified that he had seen bascarts left outside the store, sometimes in the rain or lying on their side. Ms. Martinez, an acquaintance of the Dominguez's, testified she had been shopping there and had observed the equipment used in the store. Her testimony indicates that a short time prior to the occurrence in question she had had the same trouble as Ms. Dominguez and she testified that the bascarts in the store needed "fixing up." This evidence was sufficiently relevant as to time and similarity of circumstance as to have some probative value in determining the condition of the bascarts in the store at the time of Ms. Dominguez's injury. (Citation omitted.) It tended to show not only the defective condition of the bascarts in the store at the time of the occurrence but also that Scott's knew or should have known of such condition at that time. (Citations omitted.)

The circumstantial proof in this case established more than mere neutral circumstances of control and management and tended to affirmatively establish the bent and defective condition of the bascarts. (Citations omitted.) In our opinion, it raised more than a mere surmise or suspicion of negligence. We hold that the jury could properly have concluded from the evidence that the bascarts in question were bent and defective and that Ms. Dominguez's injury was proximately caused by Scott's negligent failure to repair or replace such bascarts.

(The remainder of the opinion, dealing principally with alleged conflicts in Ms. Dominguez's testimony, with appellant's "new trial" argument, and with its "repetitious testimony" argument, is omitted.)

NOTE ON PETITION FOR REHEARING AND ON MANDATE

Defendant filed a petition for rehearing, which was denied without opinion.

Defendant then filed a motion for stay of mandate pending petition for certiorari to the Supreme Court. The "mandate," which is the order by which the appellate court transmits its decision to the trial court, was stayed pursuant to this motion, until the Supreme Court had finally disposed of the case.

E. THE SUPREME COURT

NOTE ON PETITION FOR CERTIORARI

Defendant determined that it wished to ask the Supreme Court to exercise its power of discretionary review. Chances of obtaining relief through this avenue are usually poor; the Supreme Court of the United States has many thousands of petitions for certiorari filed with it annually and grants only a very few. The petition for certiorari is similar in some respects to a brief, but its purpose and message are different: it must convince the Court that the question is of such broad significance that it should be addressed as a means of clarifying the law.

In this case, the petition for certiorari prompted the following one-sentence letter from the Clerk of the Supreme Court:

"Dear Mr. Livingston:
    "The Court today entered the following order in the above case:
        "The petition for writ of certiorari is denied.
* * *"

Mr. Livingston filed a petition for rehearing, which likewise was answered in one sentence:

"Dear Mr. Livingston:
    "The Court today entered the following order in the above case:
        "The petition for rehearing is denied.
* * *"

F. SATISFACTION OF THE JUDGEMENT

ROUGH ESTIMATE OF PRICE
PAID BY DEFENDANT
FOR ENTIRE LITIGATION

Defendant paid the judgment, with interest and costs (costs were computed at $80.50 by the District Clerk; interest finally amounted to something in excess of $3000). Note that the term "costs" means only the recoverable costs of court, which are much smaller than the parties' expenses of trial (or for that matter, the real cost of trial to the taxpayers). Total satisfaction:

$ 9,000.00

Defendant's attorney's fees are exceedingly difficult to estimate; they were probably billed on an hourly rate varying somewhere between 30 and 60 dollars per hour, depending upon factors including the year the item of work was done, the attorney doing it, the outcome of the litigation, and the volume of other work done for the client. A rough estimate would be that the services of Defendant's attorneys in this case could have exceeded $15000 but probably did not exceed $20,000:

15,000 to
20,000.00

It is customary in this situation for significant expenses to be passed on to the client. These would include printing expense for briefs ($1000 to $2000, possibly) and expenses of depositions (here, possibly $500). Therefore, a rough estimate:

2,000.00

Preparation of the record was estimated by the District Clerk at:

1,000.00

A rough total would be $25,000 to $30,000. (The comparable figure in 1975 dollars would have been about half as much.)

NOTE ON RELEASE OF JUDGMENT

At the time of furnishing its check to plaintiff's attorney, defendant received of plaintiff a document drafted by defendant's attorney, declaring that Plaintiff gave defendant a "full and final release" of the judgment. Defendant filed this document among the records of the district court.

CLOSING STATEMENT BETWEEN PLAINTIFF & HER ATTORNEY

Claimant: **MIRANDA DOMINGUEZ**
Defendant: **SCOTT'S FOOD STORES, INC.**
Total Settlement: $ **7,109.00**
Checks Out:
    Attorney fees at **40**% . . . . $ **2,843.60**
    Loans. . . . . $ _____
    Medical:
    _____ $ _____
                       $ _____

    Other Expenses:
    10% OF RECOVERY FOR $ **710.90**
    APPEAL (FEE INCLUDES ALL $ _____
    COURT COSTS, DEPOSITIONS, AND $ _____
    OTHER LEGAL EXPENSES) $ _____
Total: . . . . $ **3,554.50**
Total to Claimant: _____ $ **3,554.50**
APPROVED AND AGREED this ____ day of _____, 19 ___.

                                  Mrs. Miranda Dominguez
                                   Claimant

G. NOTES AND QUESTIONS ON THE EXPENSE OF LITIGATION

1. **THE COST OF LITIGATION TO THE LITIGANTS.** Do you find yourself surprised at the cost of the litigation? It should be added that this book does not show everything; each attorney's file was six to eight inches thick. There were briefing notes, interview notes, drafts, a mass of additional correspondence, and the like.

One way to place the case in context is to compare it mentally with one of the more complex cases in your casebook. An antitrust case, for example, may be presented in the form of an appellate opinion a few pages long in the casebook, but it may easily have involved the discovery of several million documents and required the exertion of a different kind of organizational skill by the attorneys.

Another way to view this case is to ask you to reconsider the plaintiff's attorney's decision to accept employment (considered earlier in chapter two). In a metropolitan area, it may be difficult for an attorney to justify employment in a case with less than, say, $50,000 in controversy—unless it fits a standard mold and can be adequately handled by a "clinic" approach.

2. **THE COST OF LITIGATION TO THE TAXPAYER.** Each courtroom requires a support staff in addition to the judge. Each federal district judge is entitled to two law clerks (who are usually recent law school graduates), and each generally has additional staff in the form of secretaries, courtroom deputies (who perform scheduling functions) or clerks. The court must also be supported by adequate personnel in the offices of the marshal and district clerk, not to mention such mundane services as telephone switchboarding and maintenance. In summary, the trial of a case such as Ms. Dominguez's would cost the taxpayers several thousand dollars.

3. REFORM. What do these costs, in the context of a case in which plaintiff netted just over $3500, say about our procedural system? Should that system be reformed? If so, how? By substitution of cheaper administrative remedies for "small" cases? (If so, what does this conclusion say about trial by jury?) By dispensing with the rules of evidence, allowing liberal introduction of written evidence into the record (so that live witnesses need not be summoned)? By insistence upon economy in pretrial matters such as discovery? (How?)

Perhaps the fact that more than ninety per cent of cases settle indicates that the problem is not so serious. Should we employ additional means of encouraging settlement (such as informal presentation of the case to a "stand-in" judge to give an opinion as to probable outcome)? But even settlement may not be the answer, because pretrial proceedings such as discovery represent the greatest expense in most cases.

Still another possibility is that we have simply too much litigation. Might it be a reasonable approach for a society to deny the plaintiff any recovery for an injury in these circumstances, and insist that she insure against her own damages? (That solution has in fact been adopted in the automobile context by those states that have adopted no-fault insurance.)

4. THE ATTORNEY'S SKILLS. It should be clear that attorneys need a variety of skills. They need to be good interviewers, speakers, and negotiators. They need to be efficient at preparing documents (a process that, for most attorneys, involves selective cannibalizing of existing documents more than it does original writing). They also need to be good office managers—a matter that legal education has long neglected. Efficient use of staff, equipment, machines, time, and money is as important to the litigating attorney as his legal skills.

APPENDIX:

THE REAL LAWYERS IN DOMINGUEZ V. SCOTT'S FOOD STORES— A "PEOPLE" SUPPLEMENT

THOUSANDS OF STUDENTS HAVE LEARNED ABOUT CIVIL LITIGATION by studying *The Story of a Civil Suit: Dominguez v. Scott's Food Stores.* But many of them have been left with questions about the attorneys—who they were, what their practices were like, and why they did what they did.

These questions prompted the writing of this supplement. It was intended as a formal piece of writing, but what emerged was closer to a kind of "People Magazine" format. Here, then, are interviews of the "real" Robert Livingston (Houston attorney Robert A. Rowland), the "real" United States District Judge John T. Hughes (Texas District Judge Shearn Smith), and Stephen T. Elder (who was pleased enough with the verdict to allow use of his real name).

THE DEFENSE LAWYER: ROBERT A ROWLAND, JR. OF VINSON & ELKINS. HOUSTON, TEXAS

The defense lawyer, Robert Livingston, is actually a composite of two attorneys at the firm of Vinson & Elkins. Rowland worked on the case as a beginning associate. After six years with the firm, he left to become a partner in the smaller firm of Susman, Godfrey & McGowan. Rowland received his law degree from George Washington University, and he was a law clerk to Chief Judge John R. Brown of the Fifth Circuit. The photograph shows Rob and Wick Rowland together with their daughters, Julia and Emily, at home in their living room.

Q: Were you surprised by the outcome of this case? Do you think the lady proved her lawsuit?

A: Surprised? No, I don't think it's surprising. But I thought we'd win it on appeal, frankly. I didn't think there was evidence of any act of negligence and I didn't think res ipsa applied because that shopping cart was handled by hundreds of people and it wasn't under the store's control.

Q: Is the case a familiar pattern?

A: I tried a bunch of cases like it.

Q: Why do you think the plaintiff won the jury verdict?

A: You had a woman with a severely broken wrist. It was clear that she was injured. The jury believed her. The jury liked her.

Q: Was there anything else?

A: Well, the store's own witnesses' testimony didn't exactly turn out the way it was supposed to! (Laughs.) I thought they were supposed to be our witnesses! I have to compliment Steve [Elder]. He did a good job of cross-examining them.

Q: Sometimes, students who read the book wonder why the defendant's witnesses were put on in the first place and ask whether you can't prevent that by preparing the witnesses.

A: You never know how they're going to testify until you put them on the witness stand.

Q: What kind of client was the real "Scott's Foods?" What was its attitude toward these cases?

A: They had a very fine person who handled claims, in-house. They would always pay initial medical for any person injured in a store, regardless of fault. Beyond that, my experience was that there was a great number of claims. Many of them were frivolous. And a lot of them were people who were trying to beat the store out of something.

Their attitude was to conduct discovery and settle if they could, but if they couldn't, on a reasonable basis, or if they thought the claim wasn't valid, they would try it. And if they lost and thought they shouldn't have lost, and they had a shot at turning it around, they'd appeal. But they tried a lot of cases that way.

Q: A lawyer who was handling these kinds of cases—what sort of case load would he have?

A: Insurance defense lawyers, in this kind of practice, they'd have maybe seventy-five to 250 active cases. They would be in varying degrees of seriousness. Young lawyers would have cases very much like this one.

Q: What is it like to have that sort of docket? What are the problems?

A: You have to be efficient. You have to become adept at the use of form pleadings and form interrogatories. The biggest problem is schedule conflicts. People are trying to notice you for depositions, three or four maybe at one time. And with this sort of case, the client doesn't want you to spend much time.

Q: Of course, the client is right about that.

A: Sure.

Q: You left Vinson & Elkins several years ago. Why? And what is your practice like now?

A: This firm I'm in now, I think that by the credentials of its people, it's the best firm in the State. We certainly make a lot more money that I would have if I'd stayed.

As far as my practice goes, they're almost all business cases with complex issues. They involve difficult issues of law. As I recall, there were almost no contested legal issues in that slip and fall case. In my docket now, you can't afford to leave any stones unturned, and in that slip and fall case, you almost couldn't afford to turn any at all!

Q: What's the average size of your cases today?

A: About one million dollars and up.

Q: What percentage of your time do you spend now developing law, and what percentage do you spend developing the facts?

A: I don't do much research myself. We have clerks in the firm, primarily. I'd say I spend about twenty-five percent of my time thinking about legal questions and seventy-five percent on facts, if it's possible to separate it out like that.

Q: Does our system work well to resolve a case like this one?

A: A small claim like this, no. The expense of litigation today makes a trial like this one ridiculous. In fact, Frank Evans [the judge who wrote the appellate opinion] is chairman of a committee that is developing alternate dispute resolution methods. I mean, our system produces the right outcome most of the time, and in that sense it works well, but the hideous expense makes minor dispute resolution impractical.

124

Q: In handling a case like this, how would you defend it? What sort of a jury would you want, as a defense lawyer?

A: I'd be looking for white collar, educated, intelligent, professional people. Accountants and engineers. That's about it.

You see, there was no question of the legitimacy of the injury here. Some slip-and-falls are fakes, and this one wasn't in that category. But the defendant sincerely felt that it was not at fault. It was an unavoidable accident, or attributable to something in the conduct of the plaintiff.

That being the case, you wanted intelligent tough-minded jurors who could understand that a premises owner just can't be made an insurer of anyone injured on the premises, and who would decide the case that way.

Q: What about discovery?

A: There are two purposes that people use depositions for. First, as a discovery tool, to find out. Second, to intimidate, oppress and see how far you can push the other side. You can find out how witnesses will react to anger, pressure, and confusion. But I use depositions for discovery, myself.

I guess the most important thing is to be thorough, to cover the waterfront.

Q: What about pleadings? What's the importance of pleadings?

A: I don't place too much emphasis on drafting pleadings. I used to, but I don't anymore. We have notice pleading. It's rare that pleadings make that much difference unless there's a mistake made or you leave something out.

Q: Just before trying a lawsuit, how do you feel?

A: Desperate.

Q: Why?

A: There's such great uncertainty. You have to be on your toes and ready to handle whatever might be thrown at you. You are pitted against another person in a battle of wits. A battle of preseverance. A battle of presence in front of the jury. When you're in trial, you're acting. But you know that the unexpected might happen at any moment.

Q: How does it feel to lose a jury trial?

A: It's something you never get used to. You second-guess yourself about how you could have won it. It's very hard. Takes me a long time to get over it. But it's a great feeling to win.

Q: Sort of like playing poker for a living?

A: (Laughs.) That's right.

Q: What's the down side to being a trial lawyer?

A: You have to work long hours, and at tedious work. It doesn't matter how smart you are. He who works hardest usually wins. And so you don't see your family, and they have to be very tolerant. It takes a heavy toll, it's hard work, and it's exhausting. Frankly, it's anxiety-provoking most of the time. Business litigation is especially that way, because a lot of times the law isn't clear, which makes the outcome that much more unpredictible.

Q: And so why do you do it?

A: It's the only place to be. It's what I want to do. To each his own, but I can't imagine doing anything else.

THE PLAINTIFF'S LAWYER: STEVE ELDER, SOLO PRACTITIONER, HOUSTON, TEXAS

Steve Elder was a few years out of the University of Texas Law School when he took "Mrs. Dominguez's" case. Six years later, he had done well enough to take some time off and move to the country. He was elected county attorney of rural Waller County, Texas. He had served one term in that office when he "got a bellyful of it," and he retired from litigation altogether. Today, he and his wife run a real estate title company in Katy, Texas, beyond the point where metropolitan Houston fades into the rural landscape. In the photo, Tricia and Steve Elder stand in front of the family business with their daughter, Sarah, and their son, Thomas Jefferson Elder III (known as "Jay").

Q: Why do you think you won the case? What was the biggest factor?

A: We got around an instructed verdict. We had a fair-minded judge who was inclined to let the jury decide it. With another judge, maybe a little more defense-oriented, I might have been instructed out [i.e., suffered an adverse directed verdict]. And if I'd been instructed out, I don't think I could have gotten it reversed.

Q: How important was the jury selection?

A: Picking the jury is the most important part of most trials.

Q: What were you looking for in your jury?

A: Well, I was looking for Spanish-surnamed people and the defense lawyer was looking for grocers, I'm sure. (Laughs.) I had better odds, because there are more Mexican-Americans in Houston than there are grocers, but the jury didn't have very many of either. We ended up, as I recall, with ten whites and two blacks, and with more women than men, which I thought was better for me. If I couldn't find any Mexican-Americans I at least wanted some older women. I wanted to avoid people with suits and ties. I think I ended up with only one man with a tie on.

Q: You struck the men who were wearing ties?

A: You bet.

Q: What did you find out from talking to the jury afterward?

A: We would have gotten more money if we had had the doctor there. As you know, we could only get damages for pain and suffering because we didn't lay the predicate for medical damages or loss of physical ability. The jury said they wanted to give more, but there weren't any questions in the charge about those things. And they were suspicious about the fact that the doctor wasn't there. They assumed that was because the doctor would have testified against her, even though that wasn't so at all.

Q: Why didn't you call the doctor as a witness?

A: I would have had to pay the doctor myself for his time. And my biggest fear, in the first place, was a directed verdict against me. The case was kind of a marginal case. You know, nowadays, I don't know if the lady could get a lawyer. The practice has become so specialized that a case like this would be taken by a P.I. lawyer, if at all. There are fewer and fewer "family" lawyers in the cities. It used to be, you could take a P.I. case here, a divorce there, write a will, and so forth, but not now. And if the case were taken by a P.I. specialist, he'd have paid to have the doctor there, but then again, he wouldn't have taken the case in the first place.

Q: Why did you take the case?

A: Her daughter was a client in another matter and came to me, and so I took this. I kind of halfway took it, and I thought, 'If I write a letter to them, maybe they'll pay something.' But if you take the case, you ought to spend the money to try it right, and I learned from trying this one.

Q: Obviously, you would have liked to have settled it.

A: I wanted a little bit more than the medical for her, but if they had offered me, say, one and one-half times the medical, I'd have advised her to settle and not even kept a fee.

Q: When you were trying the case, you had some evidence you wanted to get in about the condition of the carts—other carts, on other days. When the defense objected, the judge kept it out. But you kept asking about it, until the judge reversed his ruling. What was going through your mind?

A: Well, I was just trying to get the truth to the jury by getting overruled! (Laughs.) I once knew a lawyer who told that to the judge when the judge called him to the bench—"Well, judge, I'm just trying to get the truth to the jury by having you overrule my questions"—and the judge almost put him in jail.

But seriously, I had a fair-minded judge, and I figured that if I rephrased it, and got it right, so that it would hold up if the appellate court looked over his shoulder, I thought he might let it in. Good lawyers can keep doing that, asking the same question in rephrased form, for hours. It's like Chris Evert Lloyd, she's just good at hitting them from the back court, and she just keeps hitting them till the other side gets tired or gives up. It's a matter of persistence.

Q: You argued to the jury that if the lady had shopped in a rich part of town, she wouldn't have been hurt. Where'd you get the idea for that argument?

A: From Karl Marx. (Laughs.) I was trying to appeal to the middle-class conscience.

Q: Was it an appropriate argument? A proper one?

A: What do you mean? It was raised by the evidence. It was a fair inference from the evidence. You can't argue a case like this without talking about safety as versus dollars. That's what negligence law is all about.

Q: You didn't do much in the way of discovery. Why not?

A: Well, I didn't do much formal discovery, but I didn't expect that I'd find out much that way because the store's people really didn't know how it happened. I did a lot of discovery of my own case. I dug into my witnesses and I went out to the store, that kind of thing.

Q: Lawyers don't usually depose their own clients. But in this case, you asked some questions of your own client at her deposition. Why?

A: The way the deposition was going up to that point, I thought the store might ask for a summary judgment. I wanted to get just enough on the record so I could be sure a summary judgment wouldn't be granted.

Q: You could have done that by affidavit, if it came to that.

A: Yes, but it was their nickle for the deposition.

Q: You don't try cases any more, at all. Why not?

A: I outgrew it. For years, I took whatever came in the door, and I did well enough so that about 1975, I could coast. I was getting so much business I needed another lawyer. I could see I was going to be practicing law in Houston forever. It was time to get out. I went out to the country, and after a while I stumbled into getting elected county attorney. I tried maybe two drunk driving cases a month, and that lets you work up a sweat and have the fun of matching wits against somebody, but without a lot of pressure. Then I stumbled into this title insurance company and I couldn't sell it, and I got into buying real estate with title problems I thought I could cure. So now I'm a real estate speculator who owns a title company and I use the title company to clear titles.

Q: How did you feel when you were about to try a case?

A: Scared. Scared of leaving something out. Scared of doing something dumb.

THE JUDGE: HONORABLE SHEARN SMITH, 61st DISTRICT COURT OF HARRIS COUNTY, TEXAS

Judge Shearn Smith won election to the bench in 1968, against a field of six opponents. He has run unopposed ever since. Before assuming the bench, he obtained his law degree from the University of Houston and was a trial lawyer for seventeen years. Two of his four children—a son and a daughter—are trial lawyers today.

Q: You've told us you don't have an independent memory of this case, which is understandable. The average judge in this State tries 22 jury cases annually. About how many jury trials do you have each year?

A: Last year, I tried 46. I try to average about 50. Also, I try about 60 non-jury cases a year, plus ancillary matters.

Q: And during the course of a trial like the one in this book, you have to make literally dozens of decisions. Many of them are about evidence. Can you give us an idea of the kinds of problems a trial judge faces when he rules on evidence questions?

A: Essentially, you're ruling on a specific question, but often it's in relation to other questions that establish the materiality of the particular question. You have to rule at that time, and you don't have the answers to the questions that will come later.

Q: In this case, it appears you excluded certain evidence at first, and then you later admitted it. Without directing yourself to the specific questions here, can you tell us why that might happen and whether it is common?

A: Often, the attorney can approach the same piece of evidence from a different predicate base and get a different ruling. And from looking back at the record, it looks as though the language barrier was a problem in this particular case.

Q: Is this a case that "should" have been settled?

A: From a court management standpoint, an opportunity for narrowing of the issues, or settlement, should be made available to the lawyers under the guidance of a docket judge or someone other than the trial judge. Since the time of this case, we've implemented that system in this county.

Q: What are some common kinds of mistakes that you've seen lawyers make in jury trials?

A: Using lawyer language, not understood by the witness or the jury. Not reviewing the court file from front to back, reasonably close to the trial. Many attorneys assume things have been filed, but they're not there. And learning how much is too much. One question too many can hurt.

Q: This was a relatively uncomplicated case. Can you give us an idea what it's like to preside over a "bigger" or more complicated case?

A: Well, I have a case that the jury is out deliberating right now. It's a very difficult products liability case with alter ego issues, to try to reach the parent corporation. It could have taken several weeks to try. There are seven attorneys. One set of attorneys used a dolly to bring in three file cabinets of case material. It's a death case, by asphyxiation, and the complete heating system of a mobile home was put in evidence and assembled in the courtroom. We started on Monday and finished the evidence yesterday [Thursday of the same week] and had the charge prepared last night. It was argued this morning. You have to be organized enough to keep the flow in the courtroom normal, but at the same time not put undue pressure on the attorneys.

Q: The case in the book was a slip and fall case. How many slip and falls have you tried? And what advice would you give lawyers about taking them on a contingent fee basis?

A: I'd just have to say "many." In recent years, it has lessened. Make a realistic evaluation of the case, keeping in mind that you're practicing law for a living.